Busting 'Em and
Other Big League Stories

THE MCFARLAND HISTORICAL BASEBALL LIBRARY

Busting 'Em and Other Big League Stories

by Ty Cobb

WITH AN INTRODUCTION BY JOHN N. WHEELER

McFarland Historical Baseball Library, 1
Marty McGee *and* Gary Mitchem, *Editors*

McFarland & Company, Inc., Publishers
Jefferson, North Carolina, and London

Library of Congress Cataloguing-in-Publication Data

Cobb, Ty, 1886–1961.
  Busting 'em and other big league stories / by Ty Cobb ; with an
introduction by John N. Wheeler.
  [Marty McGee and Gary Mitchem, series editors]
    p. cm. — (McFarland historical baseball library ; 1)
  Ghostwritten by John N. Wheeler.
  Originally published: New York : E. J. Clode, 1914.
  Includes index.

  ISBN 0-7864-1599-1 (softcover : 50# alkaline paper)

  1. Baseball—United States—Anecdotes.   2. Cobb, Ty, 1886–
1961.   I. Wheeler, John N. (John Neville), b. 1886.   II. Title.
III. Series.
  GV873.C6   2003   2002155757

British Library cataloguing data are available

Cover image: Ty Cobb *(Classic Photos)*

Manufactured in the United States of America

McFarland & Company, Inc., Publishers
  Box 611, Jefferson, North Carolina 28640
    www.mcfarlandpub.com

Table of Contents

Editors' Note

Busting 'Em and Other Big League Stories, published in 1914 by Edward J. Clode, was the first of three books credited to Ty Cobb the author.* The book was in fact ghostwritten by *New York Tribune* sportswriter John N. Wheeler, as were the articles collected for Christy Mathewson's *Pitching in a Pinch*, published two years earlier. But *Busting 'Em* has enjoyed little of the attention or praise that the Mathewson book has, despite the tone, gentle humor, and even the ghostwriter they share. Cobb's book has instead drawn a curious ad hominem sort of criticism—Al Stump notes in *Cobb* that readers and reviewers alike commented mostly about Cobb, declaring him the more egomaniacal for having put his name to a book— and outright dismissal, the light-hearted gossip and self-effacing manner seeming too disingenuous to bother with. The book is, the argument seems to go, inauthentic.

But it may be largely as a text engaging the public in polite conversation that *Busting 'Em* is of interest today. Whether Cobb left as little to Wheeler's discretion as he did to Stump in *My Life*

---

*My Life in Baseball, Cobb's collaboration with Al Stump, would follow in 1961; his *Memoirs of Twenty Years in Baseball*, in 2002.

in Baseball, there can be little doubt that Cobb approved the book's topics and sorted judiciously through the details to be related. Both books, but particularly *Busting 'Em,* acknowledge public criticism—public misapprehension, Cobb might say—and set very earnestly about the business of "correcting" the record. This is the premeditative Cobb of legend.

And here was a man who at the height of his baseball powers (having just won the eighth of nine consecutive batting titles) was nevertheless in certain need of a new public image. Less than two years before Wheeler and Cobb undertook their collaboration, Cobb made headlines at Hilltop Park when he leaped into the stands and repeatedly punched a heckler who had all but two fingers missing. In 1909 his apparent spiking of Frank Baker nearly touched off rioting in Philadelphia. Later that season, Cobb cut and beat a nightwatchman at the Euclid Hotel in Cleveland, sending the man to the hospital and making news. Members of the St. Louis Browns and even his own teammates were reported to have conspired against him in the 1910 batting championship debacle.

It's difficult not to bear these incidents in mind while reading chapters such as "The Effect of Crowds on Big Leaguers." Buried in the middle, just after Cobb's gloss of the Baker incident, is his side of the Hilltop Park beating. Cobb recalls in detail the verbal abuse he withstood and his attempts to avoid it, the support his teammates demonstrated as he charged the stands, and even the umpire's reluctance to eject him for the offense. Memory of the beating itself has gone missing: "As I sit and try to recall the incidents of the next few minutes, they are all vague and hazy to me." The reader is left to conclude that either Cobb was so sorely provoked that he was unconscious to all but his rage, and so not answerable for the beating; or Cobb, deeply unsettled by the event, repressed the memory of it. He evades blame either way.

Editors' Note

Suggestions of historical revision abound in the book. In "Facing Tough Breaks in the Big Leagues," for instance, Cobb relates a clubhouse incident from his rookie season, 1905. After a Tiger "fielder" mishandles a double play chance that may have cost the Tigers the game, he is set upon by his teammates, including Cobb, who writes, "We all went after that player." A volley of accusation is followed by the fielder's recriminations: "If you guys had made as many hits as I did to-day, we would have taken [the game]" and "How am I going to hit them with anyone on, if you fellows can't reach the bags?" Cobb himself was quick to criticize the performance and skills of others; one begins to wonder how closely Cobb identifies with the fielder, whom he describes as having been "put on the rack." And when the player, called "yellow," physically attacks his accuser, Cobb explains, "'Yellow' is a fighting word in the Big Leagues." But the row is nothing serious, and team unity and camaraderie prevail: "After a few cold baths, we cooled off"; things were "patched up." Personal attacks were the common manifestation of stress and could only temporarily strain team relations.

But the reader knows that Cobb was an outcast by late in his first season, and it is unlikely that he would have been welcome even in the easy company of a mob. As Cobb told Al Stump, "It was a them-against-me setup.... It wasn't about to get better." By 1914, Cobb's estrangement from his teammates was familiar to many who followed the game. Whether Cobb here recasts his own ostracism, spinning it for his own or the public's benefit, is an open question, but one that intrigues.

Whatever Cobb intended *Busting 'Em* to be or do, it has had no effect on the way he is remembered. The book, long out of print and difficult to find, is seldom listed in the bibliographies that accompany Cobb biographical capsules on the Internet and in reference works. It is also missing from Charles Alexander's *Ty Cobb*, possibly the most punctilious and highly regarded among the biographies. Even John N. Wheeler's obituary in the *New York Times*, which names the many celebrities he collaborated with or syndicated, including Christy Mathewson, makes no mention of either the book or of Cobb.

But *Busting 'Em*, with all that it suggests about Cobb the person and all that it tells about the player's baserunning and hitting strategies, is fascinating. We're proud to make it available once more to serious fans of the game.

Marty McGee
Gary Mitchem

Introduction

Did you ever hear anyone ask:

"Who is 'Ty' Cobb?"

If you did, you have discovered a very isolated case. Cobb is known far and wide by all followers of baseball and by the few in these United States who are not followers of the game. He is an institution in baseball like the Presidency of the United States is in politics. He is the man that folks expect to lead both Big Leagues in batting each season, and he always makes good, or at least he has for the past several seasons, as long as he has been working at leading the league.

Among other things, Cobb is the greatest base runner that baseball ever produced. He makes lightning look slow, for he is a speed flash. He is the fastest thinker in the game, too, and the fans delight to see him make some rival player, who is not as fast as Cobb intellectually, look foolish.

Besides being a mechanical marvel in execution, "Ty" Cobb is the most sensational player the game has ever produced, and he is always doing the unexpected, taking long chances and big risks at being injured. In short, Cobb is concentrated baseball, a bunch of live-wire nerves.

Introduction by John N. Wheeler

But the "Terrible Ty" is not of the ordinary type off the field, either. He has improved the opportunities which baseball has presented to him and so has devoted considerable time to writing stories for newspapers and magazines. Cobb is a born reporter and would have been a star in the newspaper business if he had adopted that line of work instead of baseball. He can absorb information rapidly and set down his impressions easily and graphically. He is an intellectual blotter.

Cobb has covered his Big League career very thoroughly in this book, *Busting 'Em and Other Big League Stories,* and he has filled it full of anecdotes bearing on men whose names are famous in baseball. In short, he has devoted his winter to setting down in a breezy way the high spots of his experiences and connection with the game and its stars. He has given the readers the real "inside" of life in the Big Leagues and baseball as it is played in fast society.

Readers: Meet Mr. "Ty" Cobb, author.

John N. Wheeler

◆ CHAPTER I ◆

Busting 'Em

When a Big Leaguer is hitting the ball hard, the rest of his team says:—

"That's busting 'em."

I had trouble learning to hit, and so I made a study of the styles of other batters. Lajoie and Jackson are natural free swingers, Speaker and Collins, scientific hitters. How "Joe" Jackson twice ran out on the Athletics. Other inside gossip on the peculiarities of batting stars.

To "Willie" Keeler is attributed the authorship of the golden rule of batting, and I suppose he said it. When somebody asked "Willie" a long time ago how he kept his batting average above three hundred right along, he replied:

"Hit 'em where they ain't."

The prescription has stuck to baseball like a canker sore to an engaged girl's lip. Its very truth has been responsible for its long life, and the saying will probably last as many years as the game itself. There is no doubt in my mind that "Bob" Fitzsimmons' immortal "The bigger they are the harder they fall" will be repeated in prize fight stories as long as any man pulls on a glove. I don't know whether "Bob" said that or not but he gets credit for it, which amounts to the

I get up and write them down do I won't forget them.

same thing. I am sorry that I have never been able to spring any-thing in connection with baseball with a punch in it which would live long after my name had been forgotten, or, at least, to have received the credit for some pithy remark. But, if the field were still open and there were no quotations about Keeler's "Hit 'em where they ain't," I honestly believe I would have pulled that one because it has always been my idea in batting.

Nearly all the great hitters of to-day are those who place their punches or bat behind the runner. There are few of the old style sluggers left, the men who just take a long, healthy wallop at the ball and trust that it will not go up against some fielder. Most of the boys in the select "three hundred" class are using their heads all the time they are at the plate to outguess the fielders and the opposing pitcher and stand them all on their heads. This style of hitting gives a player what we call the "percentage," or the edge, and every man who is to bat up over three hundred needs this "percentage."

Each year Big Leaguers hear players on their circuit grumbling because they declare they are hitting every ball on the nose, but that it is going straight to a fielder.

"I can't get any of the breaks with my wallops," they complain.

It is not tough luck, but rather they are not playing the game with their heads. Only one really great hitter of modern baseball has gotten away with this careless, free swinging style. That man is "Joe" Jackson, the great slugger of the Cleveland club, the player who crowded me so hard for the batting championship last season. "Joe" just busts them and hopes for the best. He has a wonderful eye and great natural strength. He is a born hitter, and that is the reason he gets away with it. Men like Collins, Baker, and myself are developed batters and must be scientific in our work. I would hate to think how much Jackson could hit if he began to figure on getting the "percentage."

For a long time "Doc" White, of the Chicago White Sox, had the edge on me because I could not connect with his curve ball, and he would continue to hand me curve after curve until he curve-balled me to death. I kept figuring on a way to overcome this weakness, because it was leaving big cavities in my batting average that worried me every time I faced "Doc." I was sitting in the lobby of a hotel in Chicago one night after dinner fretting over this thing when suddenly I jumped up and shouted to no one in particular:

"I've got it!"

"Got what?" asked "Wild Bill" Donovan, who was sitting next me and looking over a list of pitching averages in the newspaper. He acted as if he thought I had just jarred a screw loose in my dome.

"I've got the way to hit that curve ball of 'Doc' White's," I replied.

"You need it," answered "Bill," and went on with his pitching averages.

The next time White worked against us I could hardly wait for my turn at bat to try out my new theory. Heretofore, I had been standing up in the front of the batter's box, and his curve would break just as the ball reached me. I had no chance to gauge it. Suddenly it came to me that, if I moved to the back of the box, I would get the curve after it had broken and have a chance to gauge it.

Of course, when I faced "Doc" he began to work his old curve, and I let the first one go by to see how it looked from my new point of view. It looked good to me. Then he wasted one and came back at me with the curve. I hit the ball on a line over second base. Ever since then I have been able to whang "Doc" White's pitching, and I haven't known that he has a curve ball. I am sorry to see that he is out of the league, for he has been a soft spot for me. All that was necessary was to get the ball after the curve had broken so I could gauge it.

Following this discovery, I have stood toward the back of the batter's box for all left-handers and find it easier to hit a southpaw from this position. For right-handers I move up to the front of the batter's box and get their curve, as a rule, before it breaks.

If you listen carefully, many catchers will tip a batter off to what to expect by their conversation. They try to be wise, but from what they say you can often guess the sort of ball the pitcher will throw. For instance, I know a catcher in our league who thinks it is great shrewdness to keep repeating the count on the batter. I am not going to mention his name because it might tip him off, and he would naturally quit the practice. His favorite situation for this trick is with two strikes and nothing. He got away with it on me two or three times before I caught on. With two and nothing on a batter, the pitcher generally figures to waste one, hoping to get the hitter to swing at a bad ball. As a general thing he will shoot one across your neck, the hardest place for most men to connect.

"Two strikes," said this catcher one day when I was at the bat. "Come on, now. Two strikes and nothing." His talk was supposed to be aimed at the pitcher, but was really for my benefit.

I was looking for one around the neck, when the twirler shot a fast one over the plate, waist high, a perfect strike, and I fanned. I made a mental note that the next time I would be watching for this. It wasn't until the following series with this club that the same situation arose, and then the catcher came out with his:

"Come on, now. Two strikes and nothing. Get this guy."

Sure enough, the next ball came up the groove, and I kissed it for three bags. He has not tried to be wise with me recently. So it will be seen that batting is something besides just hitting the ball.

On the whole, I do not consider the catchers of to-day to be as wise and tricky as those who were working when I first broke into the league. It is probably because the game has developed so rapidly and the catcher is forced to carry more matter on his mind. He is always watching base runners and has several signs to keep in his head besides the battery signals. He must be on the lookout for hit-and-run signs given by the opposing team, in order to break up the play with a pitchout, and he has many other duties. If he attempts to trick a batter, he is liable to slip up himself.

"Nig" Clarke, of the old Clevelands, used to pull one that bothered me a good deal when I was first in the league. After giving his sign, he would reach down and grab up a handful of dirt as if to dry the sweat off his hands. Then, just when the ball came up to the plate, he would throw this dirt on the batter's feet. The action naturally distracted a man's attention and took his mind off the pitch. In other words, Clarke was working on the batter's nerves. There can be no success in batting without concentration. "Jack" O'Connor, the old catcher, had a habit of talking continuously to worry the hitters. His favorite play was to shove his glove up around your neck, where you couldn't help but see it, and wave it there, saying:

"Come one. Put one up here."

Of course, he would cross you and the ball would not come around the neck. But the waving glove, which could be seen just out of the tail of the eye, would make you sore and want to bat it. He would keep his glove there until the ball had almost reached him, too, in order to disconcert his victim. But the strictness of the umpires at the present time and the great number of signs it is now necessary for a catcher to remember, make it almost impossible for them to practice tricks on hitters.

Old "Billy" Sullivan, catcher of the White Sox, used to be a wonder at figuring out batters and then crossing them. He slipped one over on Lajoie toward the end of the season of 1908 which practically knocked Cleveland out of the pennant that year and gave the flag to Detroit. That is why I heard the play discussed so often and why I attach so much importance to it. At this time to which I refer, Chicago, Cleveland, St. Louis, and Detroit were all bunched for the pennant. Cleveland looked best, while St. Louis was about to crack, and the White Sox still had a chance.

In the final game of the last series of the season between Chicago and Cleveland, the late "Addie" Joss was working against "Ed" Walsh at his best. The White Sox had a lead of one run, but the Naps had managed to get three men on the bases in the last inning of the game. Two were out when Lajoie came to the bat as the final hope of Cleveland. It was a ticklish situation, and Walsh and Sullivan went to work carefully on the great slugger.

Lajoie always had some difficulty in hitting Walsh's spitters, so "Big Ed" fed him a couple, and he pulled them down the lines for hard drives, but each a few feet foul. The count on Lajoie was finally narrowed down to three balls and two strikes, with the game and maybe the pennant depending on that next pitch. Sullivan signed for a fast ball, but Walsh shook his head. He had great faith in his spitter when it was right, as it was that day, and he desired to place the burden on the spitball and take a chance on it going wide of the plate and losing his man and perhaps the game. A spitter is hard to control, but Walsh did not figure Lajoie would let it go if the ball was at all close to being a strike.

After Walsh had shaken his head to the sign for a fast one, Sullivan came back at him with it, and once more Walsh shook his head to mean no. Sullivan would not give in and handed the spitball pitcher the fast-ball sign for the third time. At last Walsh conceded it. He bluffed at wetting the ball and wound up, with all three men on the bases on the move, but it shot across the plate at Lajoie's knees and fooled the big Frenchman, who had been looking for a spitter and expected the ball to break bad, when he saw how low it was coming. He thought it would surely be a ball, and it would have been had Walsh thrown a spitter at the same height as Lajoie figured he would.

During the progress of the discussion between Walsh and Sullivan on the kind of ball to give Lajoie in the crisis, a conversation carried on by means of signs, the batter had been figuring this way: Sullivan had probably asked for a fast one, and Walsh had shaken his head. "Billy" had repeated his request for a fast one, but Walsh had shaken his head a second time. Then again, and Walsh had nodded that the sign suited him. Sullivan had given in, so thought

Lajoie, and Walsh would throw the spitter. He figured on the wrong man giving in, and his miscalculation cost Cleveland the game. If the pitch had been a spitball, as Lajoie figured, he would have gotten a base on balls, a run would have been forced home, and the score would have been tied. His dope was wrong. That was all. Nothing was lacking about his mechanical execution. There never is with Lajoie. He has the greatest natural form in baseball to my mind, but I will have more to say about that later in this series.

"Joe" Jackson is also a wonderful natural batter. He was ripe when he first came up to the Big League and joined the Athletics in 1908. Jackson was born a sticker, has always been ripe since he has been strong enough to swing a bat, and will be able to "bust 'em" long after his legs and arms wear out. It is the way with all men of his type. They retain their batting ability after their other Big League qualities have been frayed out. Look at "Mike" Donlin, and even Lajoie, who is beginning to slow up on his legs, but who wings the ball as hard as ever.

But Jackson, to my mind, loses a lot of hits he would get if he studied out the game. For instance, he cannot tell anyone else how to bat. He doesn't know himself how he hits, or when he is going to hit, or where he will hit the ball.

Few fans are acquainted with Jackson's personal history and the story of how he broke into the Big League. He was born in Greenville, S.C., which is not very far from my home, where he worked in the cotton mills, a business that does not permit much opportunity for obtaining an education. "Shoeless Joe" began playing ball on the side, however, and built up such a reputation as a sticker that "Connie" Mack, whose ears are sensitive when some fellow is drilling out long hits in the bushes, heard about him and brought him up to the Athletics. "Connie" was stuck on the solid style in which Jackson stung the ball, and when he found that "Joe" had overlooked getting an education, he offered to provide it for him.

"Joe" had always been used to the cotton mills and the life in the South, and he grew homesick after being with the Athletics for a short time, becoming restless, too, because he did not get a chance to work regularly. He complained to Mack about this.

"Wait," said "Connie," who likes to teach all his ball players to be patient like himself. "This is your big chance."

"But I want to play every day or else go back South," answered "Joe."

"But you must get Big League habits first," replied the careful "Connie."

It was not much more than a week after this that the Athletics were playing a series in Washington. One day Jackson was missed from the bench.

"Has anybody seen 'Joe' Jackson? Is he sick?" asked "Connie."

"I was with him last night down near the Union Station, and he said he was going to buy a newspaper," spoke up a player who is now hopelessly buried in the minors. "I trailed along, but, instead of buying a newspaper, he went to the ticket booth and got a ticket to Greenville. The last I saw of him he was going on board a train."

"That's right. Yesterday was pay-day," remarked "Connie."

Jackson evidently estimated Washington to be the nearest point to Greenville that he would touch on the Big League circuit and decided to jump the club there and get back home. He is one of the few players that have declared themselves out of the Big League. On the following day "Connie" Mack sent this telegram to Greenville:

"Join the club in Philadelphia at once if you don't want to be suspended."

Back came this reply, collect:

"Don't want to stay in the Big League. Am tired of it."

"Connie" Mack did not despair. He brought Jackson up once more through a special envoy, and this time he induced the promising and hard-hitting recruit to include his wife in the party. But again Jackson longed for the cotton-mill country, and he soon jumped the team to play in the South Atlantic League, which he led as a hitter. He could bat just as well then as he can now, or practically as well. Cleveland grabbed the slugger after Mack had relinquished all claim to him as hopeless, and "Joe" has stuck with the Naps. He is a great hitter, one of the greatest in the game. But still I believe Jackson would have been a bigger success under "Connie" Mack than he is to-day, because the wise Philadelphia leader has the knack of developing hitters and getting the best out of a man there is in him, and more. He would have taught Jackson some science in batting. That would have helped him immensely.

I consider Baker to be more dangerous than Jackson, for instance, because Baker will hit right. He has been instructed how to do this by Mack. With the shortstop covering to get a man at second, Baker will hit right, that is, he will try to drill the ball through the hole left in the infield, and almost any kind of a batted ball will get by if properly aimed at the cavity. Whereas, with the shortstop covering on the hit and run, Jackson goes after the ball just the same as he does with the bases clear. In other words, he is not a scientific hitter, and the work of a man like Baker is more valuable to a team.

Jackson is what we call a streak hitter. He bats like a fiend for a time and then his work drops off. For instance, he did most of his hitting at home last summer and very little on the road. It is difficult for him to get out of a slump. He doesn't know how and just swings harder at the ball, which usually results in a longer slump. Extra-base hits often make a batter slump and streaky in his work, and Jackson gets many of these. This may sound funny to the reader, but

I know long slams have this effect on my work. If I think I am just meeting the ball and get a home run, I am surprised.

"I didn't hit that one hard," I'll say to myself. "The next time I'll take a healthy swing at it and show them how far I can drive it."

This hard swinging tangles up the form and gets the eye off the ball. I have seen the last three world's series as a spectator, and I believe it was the state of mind to which I referred above and nothing else that was responsible for the Giants' poor showing at the bat. Men who have seen them play throughout the season tell me that the New York batters are naturally chop hitters, as are most of those in baseball nowadays. But in the world's series the Giants were all taking terrific swings at the ball, which undoubtedly threw them into the slump that attacked the team in the last three starts in the big series.

Slumps certainly worry a batter. I believe they are responsible for all the gray hairs there are in my head. It is a battle to get out of them, and I would rather slump on the road than at home, because I like opposition, and I can get myself straightened out with the crowd hooting me for failing to hit. My method of curing myself is to shorten up on the bat, so as not to overswing, and to get one of the extra pitchers out in practice and let him throw nothing but fast balls. In this way I get my eye back on the pill by trying to meet every one of them squarely and drive them to the pitcher. I do not attempt to hit hard. This results in a return of confidence, and then I begin to use more strength until I am stinging them on a line. After that, a curve does not look tough to you. A symptom of a slump in my hitting is an uncomfortable feeling when I am at the plate. If a man does not feel right in his batting position, he knows something is wrong with his work. Of course, the big thing, in overcoming a slump, is confidence and the belief that you can hit the ball.

One-field hitters slump more frequently than those who can drive the ball to any part of the diamond. By this I mean that a player who bats to left field constantly, or to any other one field, generally slumps oftener, and this is due to the fact that the fielders learn how to play for him. "Stuffy" McInnis, of the Athletics, for instance, is a left-field hitter of the most chronic type. He does most of his batting early in the spring before the pitchers get up to their best form and before the fielders are as fast as they become later. Of course, when the pitchers get good control, they keep the ball on the outside of the plate for McInnis, who is a right-handed batter, and he cannot very well pull these to left field. McInnis has another peculiarity which is well known around the American League circuit. He is a great man to hit the star pitchers, the ones with the big names and the reputations. It is against these that he does most of his batting, while with some scarcely known dinky pitcher working he is liable to look like a "sucker."

Slumps make players superstitious, nearly all men in baseball believing in luck, although most of them refuse to admit it. I know that when I am going good I always try to do everything just the same way as when I ran into the hitting streak. For instance, I always go to the park by the same route and put on my uniform the same way. Perhaps I have had a good afternoon on the preceding day, and I try to recall which sock I donned first. I remember it was my left, and I would not give the right one precedence for a raise in pay. I hang up my towel on the same peg.

I recall a row I had with the trainer of the Detroit team one day back in the season of 1909. Four hits out of five had been my record, and I carefully put my towel on the same peg where it had been when the big batting had begun. The next day when I got to the park it was on a different hook.

"Who moved by towel?" I bawled, for I was sore.

I. Busting 'Em

"I did," answered the club trainer. "It fell down, and I picked it up and hung it there."

"Why didn't you put it back on the hook where it was?" I asked peevishly, for those long seasons of batting wear on the nerves.

"I didn't know which one it was," he replied.

That afternoon I did not get a hit and blamed it on the misplaced towel. My run of luck had been broken by it. After my bath that day the towel was placed back on the old lucky peg and I "busted 'em" for fair the next afternoon.

Many fans have asked me why I always swing three bats. Originally it was my intention to make the one bat feel lighter when I went to the plate, and this practice has developed the muscles of my shoulders and back wonderfully, because the three sticks weigh approximately one hundred and twenty ounces. But I have had great luck in hitting while swinging three bats, and I would not give it up now at any price. Aside from the superstition of it, I believe the juggling of three bats, while waiting for my turn, has done me a lot of good, since it has developed me from a rather slight build to a player who is very strong in the back and arms, which strength enables me to drive the ball.

As I hinted earlier in this article, "Connie" Mack is a great manager to develop batters. The Athletics' leader is a close student of hitters and can discover their weaknesses and point them out with infallible accuracy. Star hitters cannot be made, but a man with latent possibilities can be turned into a star under the Mack tuition. When Oldring first came to the Athletics he was bad on a curve ball, and Mack got after him until now "Rube" hits up around three hundred year after year. Baker has been greatly improved since he joined the Athletics. He wasn't always the slashing sticker he is to-day.

This brings me to another thing. The great slugging of Baker in the world's series of 1911 and this year has led to many discussions

♦ 19 ♦

of his weakness. Some experts declare he has not any "groove." This may be true, but I know he is bad on a slow ball. Dubuc, who carries one of the best slow balls I ever saw, can make Baker look foolish almost every time he works for Detroit against Mack's club. The trouble with the Giant pitchers was that they fed Baker speed—that is, they did until Mathewson, the greatest student of batters that ever lived, discovered that Baker would bite at a slow one. The Trappe slugger did not get many hits off the Giant star after that. But he inhales speed. He eats it, too. I happened to be standing near the New York bench just before the first game of the 1913 world's series, and heard Matty talking to Marquard.

"Whatever you do," urged "Big Six," "Don't hand Baker a fast one. Keep them slow curves and low."

But Marquard was so nervous he did not know what he was pitching when he got out there in the box, and he slipped Baker a fast one on the inside, with the result that Baker pulled it into the right-field stand for a home run.

The first time I saw "Eddie" Collins play, which was in 1906, when he was appearing with the Athletics under the name of "Eddie" Sullivan and was still in college, he did not look like a hitter. To-day he is probably the most dangerous in baseball, as his work in the 1913 world's series showed. I consider him to be far more valuable to a team than Jackson or even Baker. He is a wonderfully scientific batter and takes advantage of every flaw of the defense, driving the ball at holes in the infield when a baseman goes to cover, and frequently outguessing the outfielders by placing his drives. Collins also has developed great form, as is shown by the speed at which he pushes out the ball. He is not physically robust, yet he gets his whole body into his swing in such a way that the drives go from his bat like a rifle-shot. He busts them as hard as any man in the league, I believe.

I. Busting 'Em

Harry Davis, once weak with the stick, became a dangerous batter under "Connie" Mack. Barry was no batter at all when he joined the Athletics, but now he is one of the best on the team in a pinch. "Jimmy" Walsh was known as a "sucker" on a curve ball at first, but under Mack he got so he could hit curves better than fast ones, although he is not a great batter yet. And so the Athletics go.

This batting strain year after year is too much of a good thing, especially when you are fighting to hold the lead in the league. Few persons realize the tension that this keeps a man under, and I am usually "crabbing" from the beginning to the end of the season. I get worse as the thing goes along, and more of my hair falls out each summer. I'll soon be entirely bald, and then they can try out some hair restorer on me. I am often asked which pitchers are hardest for me to hit. Walter Johnson always looks tough to me, and Ford is also effective.

Another feature of this fight for the batting lead of the league is that the public will not give a man any rest. You have got to keep on going whether you are sick or not, because otherwise the spectators will say you are quitting. I played for a week in 1911 with a fever of 104. A man goes through a whole lot to attain the hitting championship. If you are hurt and laid off for a few days because of the injury, you must get back in the lineup as soon as you are fit to hobble around and put on a uniform or the newspapers and fans will holler. They won't give you a chance to get your eye on the ball again before going back into the game. They'll say you are laying off because you are lazy, and that you are all right.

In fighting for the batting leadership I play all sorts of tricks to get the percentage in my favor. For instance, I try to bluff the third baseman in with an attempted bunt and then lam one down past him. If you feint the infield out of position, any kind of a hit ball goes through. But with the infielders in their places, you've got to meet the ball solidly to get away with it. My notion is to keep them all on their toes and always guessing.

This is the style of nearly all good hitters. Speaker is a great man to cross up the opposing infield. I have already mentioned Collins. These two depend largely on science for their averages, and both are stars of the first water. Lajoie and Jackson do not play the batting game so closely. They are free swingers. Lajoie always shuffles up to the plate as much as to say to the pitcher:

"Shoot one up here and see if you can get it by me."

I am constantly figuring on new ways to outguess the other side and add a hit or two to my string. Some of my best ideas have come to me at night just before I fall asleep, when, they say, great poems often come to their authors. I get up and write them down so I won't forget them, the baseball ideas, not the poems.

♦ CHAPTER II ♦

The Effect of Crowds
on Big Leaguers

Some stars are irritated by the fans. A foreign crowd makes me play harder. The real story of why I went into the bleachers in New York to punish an abusive rooter. Various threats other Big Leaguers and I have received. How I once thought I had been shot in Philadelphia when an automobile tire exploded.

Probably no Big League ball player has had as much experience with crowds as I have. Once, I went into a grand stand because a fan irritated me beyond endurance by the names he called me, and again I was threatened with being shot if I played in Philadelphia after the time I unfortunately spiked Frank Baker.

The crowd makes the ball game. How much pepper, how much enthusiasm, and how much baseball do you suppose a player would show if games were played to empty seats? Probably nearly every spectator who has ever attended a Big League contest has noticed that he sees the best baseball when the crowd is biggest and players work harder because they want to show the spectators, if they are rooting for them, that they are there, and, if the rooters are against them, they want to show that this doesn't make any difference with

"I would like to have the playing field entirely surrounded by a bunch of excitable, wild 'nuts.'"

their playing. Many Big Leaguers claim that the crowd and its rooting has no effect on them. This is not generally true. I know it has a big effect on me. Most ball players, however, like to give the impression that they are indifferent to the roasts or applause of the crowd.

The two worst towns on the American League circuit for rooters "riding" visiting ball players are St. Louis and Philadelphia.

With their club generally a tailender and hopelessly out of the race, there does not appear to be any occasion for the fans of St. Louis to be so rabid, but it seems as if about half of the spectators that go to the ball park there attend the game for the fun of panning the visiting players. The names that the occupants of the bleachers call the outfielders could not be printed on asbestos paper. If they ever get a winner in St. Louis, every visiting ball player will have to have police protection each time the home club loses a close game.

The sentiment of the Philadelphia fans is easier to understand, because they have a winning club to support, but still it is unusual, since, otherwise, Philadelphia is a nice, quiet, well behaved city where the citizens go to bed early. After I was accused of deliberately trying to spike Baker when the Athletics were fighting for the flag back in 1910, I received numerous letters telling me that I would be badly treated the next time the Tigers played in Philadelphia. The spiking incident occurred in Detroit. One of these communications stated positively, that if I played in the next series, I would be shot by a man standing on top of one of those houses outside the right field fence, the roofs of which raise themselves over the inclosure so that it would be an easy shot for anyone used to a rifle. Here is the letter:

"Ty Cobb.

"Detroit Baseball club.

"If you play against Philadelphia, you will be shot from one of the buildings outside the park. We know you are yellow because you showed it when you spiked Baker. Now let's see if you're game enough to play in that next series. If you do, you are done."

Mrs. Cobb did not want me to play, but I figured that the writer was bluffing and was just trying to scare me so that I would stay out of the lineup and weaken the team, and, anyway, I could not afford to remain out of the game. So I worked through the series, but I made no pretense of bravery for my action. It would have required more courage for me to stay out of the game, because most of the newspapers had printed stories about the letter at the time, and I would have been called "yellow" by all followers of the sport if I had not played. I would rather take a chance on being shot than have that epithet applied to me. I do not want to pose as a hero in this incident and will freely admit that I spent several uncomfortable minutes during the series in my exposed position in center field.

I recall that, in the second contest of the series, I was beginning to get used to the idea that some "bug" might be crazy enough to pot me in the back during the game, when there suddenly came a report like that made by a gun from the outside of the park behind the right field fence. I must have jumped about eight feet, for "Sam" Crawford, playing in right field, yelled at me:

"What's the matter, 'Ty'?"

"What was that?" I shouted back to him.

"Some guy blew an automobile tire outside the right-field fence," he replied. The message brought me great relief. If you don't believe this noise will scare you, try standing out there with the idea in your mind that a sharpshooter is making you his target and let someone blow a shoe. It is no nerve tonic.

The fans of Philadelphia have always "ridden" me hard, probably because I have had trouble there from time to time, and I generally play my best ball against the Athletics. I like opposition from the crowd. It makes me work harder. I once broke up in Philadelphia the longest batting slump I ever experienced after having gone to the bat seventeen times without getting a hit. I was nearly "nutty" after the seventeenth appearance, when we went along to Philadelphia the next day to play a series. The fans had been reading in the newspapers about my long slump, and the crowd was out at the park ready to "ride" me. The first time I went to the bat it seemed as if every spectator in the park joined in the chorus of that time-honored chant:

"Strike him out! Strike him out!"

The first one that Plank, who was pitching for the Athletics, threw was a curve, and I let it go. Then I set myself for a fast one, guessed it right, hooked the ball, and drove a three-bagger to right field on an inside ball. When I stopped at third base, the crowd was cheering instead of jeering, but I remembered how they had been hollering "Strike him out!" before I went to the bat, and I just waved my hands in derision at them to show then I did not care what they thought. That is why the fans call me a "bug" on the field and I, in return, call them in the stand "bugs." Nervous energy and the crowd will make a ball player do many a queer thing, but there would be no game without a crowd. Because the crowd is with you when you are going good and knocking you when things are not breaking right, I seldom take off my cap if they cheer me for a possible good play. Many Big Leaguers feel the same way in the matter. I have heard Matty say:

"Yes, they yell for me now because I struck those two men out, but they will pan me just as much in the next inning if the other boys get two or three hits off my delivery. What's the use in taking off the cap?"

Most managers appreciate the psychology of crowds now and play on the feelings of the spectators to help keep their teams at a high pitch. For instance, it used to be customary for Big League players on opposing clubs to mix up in the preliminary practice before games and act friendly. Several smart leaders have laid down the law that none of their men is to speak or shake hands with a member of an opposing team while he is in uniform. Frank Chance, new to the American League, was the most insistent during his first summer in our organization that his men carry out this injunction, and I know three or four members of the New York American League team who were fined for disregarding it.

"You are ball players and not society dancers at a pink tea," I heard Chance remark to one of his men last season after the latter had come over to our side of the field to "mitt" a Detroit player. "You are paid to come out here and play ball, and you've been doing very little of it lately. I want to see some fight in you and not this social stuff. That handshake will cost you $10, and the next one I catch you pulling will mean $25 out of your pay envelope."

McGraw, they tell me, is also against players mixing up before a game because he wants to see fight in his men, and this hand-shaking stuff is no indication of a determined spirit. Nor does the crowd like to see the opposing teams hobnobbing. It always enjoys watching players at loggerheads. Nearly all the Big League managers are opposed to the brotherly love actions now.

Many stories have gone out about the row I got into with the fan in New York. I want to tell for the first time over my signature the real inside facts of that event. This same fellow had been both-ering me on previous trips when the Detroit club had been in New York, and I was forced to work hard to hold in my temper, but had put his abuse down to the ordinary ravings of the fan who likes to believe he is tormenting a ball player. On the day in question, though, he singled me out and shouted remarks at me which could be heard all over that section of the bleachers where he sat each time I passed the stand on the way to the bench. My temper began to go, but I did my best to control it. Other members of the Detroit team got the remarks aimed at me, too, and began to get sore.

"Did you hear what that guy said?" I asked "Sam" Crawford, after a particularly vile rain of abuse in the third or fourth inning.

"I certainly did," replied "Sam," "and I would not let him get away with it, either."

"We're all behind you if you go after him," said the rest of the men on the Detroit bench.

"I guess I'll try to pass it up for a time and see if he won't quit," I answered.

II. The Effect of Crowds on Big Leaguers

In order to get the abusive one a chance to forget about it, I purposely did not come to the bench when the Detroit club went to the bat for the next inning because I had been one of the last hitters in the previous session, and it would not be my turn. I hung around the outfield and avoided getting within earshot of the man. But on the way to the bench in the following inning, when I was due to bat, I was forced to pass the left field bleachers, where he was sitting. It seemed as if he had been letting his imagination run profanely wild during the time I was in the outfield, for he heaped a particularly vile volley on me as I passed him. Nothing could have stopped me then. My temper has always been quick, and, when younger, it got me in a lot of trouble, but, in later years, I have exercised great control over it, realizing that it was a handicap and dangerous to me. But now an old flash of temper seized me and no power would have kept me out of the stand even if I had known that every fan in it was armed with a repeating rifle, and there was not a chance of me coming back alive. This is not courage, and do not think I am trying to create the impression it is, or claim any hero stuff for myself. It was simply blind fury, stirred in me by what this man with the loud voice who had singled me out, said.

As I sit and try to recall the incidents of the next few minutes, they are all vague and hazy to me. I remember starting for the front of the stand, vaulting it, and struggling up through the group of fans until I found my man, who was trying to shrink away from me, because he never thought that a ball player would come into the crowd. I next recall coming down over the bleacher seats again, while the crowd around my man gaped at me in amazement, with the spectators in the other parts of the stands on their feet in wonder, not knowing what had happened, and the Detroit players, headed by "Sam" Crawford, standing in belligerent attitudes directly in front of the stand ready to help in case anyone tried to lay a hand on me.

None did. And the odd thing is that I have no recollection of the important part of the incident, that of beating up my abuser.

As soon as I got on the field the umpire told me I was out of the game, which he had to do according to the rules of the league. He acted apologetically about it. The Detroit players, all muttering darkly over the incident, went back to the bench and laid aside the bats most of them had been carrying. I heard Jennings say:

"I knew he was going to do it. Once I got the look in his eye, I was sure of it, but there was no chance of stopping him. When he is that way, nothing would stop him." Jennings meant me and he knew me.

Of course, all readers of baseball news recall what followed that incident, the strike of the Detroit players and the sensational stories that came out of Philadelphia when none of the Tigers showed up for the Saturday game with the Athletics. Then the club was reinstated, I was punished, and the incident was smoothed over. I got back home with the club, and there came a warning by letter from a friend of mine in New York that the friends of the man I had attacked were preparing to "get" me. According to this information, his regular companions had bad reputations, and their methods were rough, some even having pictures in a well known gallery. I was told to be on my guard the next time the Tigers returned to New York, and this written warning came from no sensationalist, but from a newspaper man who had been tipped off by a Big League manager.

The threat worried me, as it probably would any other man. I recognized that I was stacked up against a bad lot, and I took certain means to protect myself when next I was in New York, and did not walk in any dark streets alone. Only once did I believe a man was following me, and now I think this impression may have been due to my imagination. It was in the subway one night, and, instead of retreating, I showed my "shadow" that he would not do himself any good by starting anything.

I regret the entire incident, because it is the only real trouble I ever had with a fan while on the ball field.

But the fans, as a class, are very decent when you come in direct contact with them. You used to hear some ball players complaining whenever there was an overflow crowd on the field because they said extra spectators interfered with their work. I have always liked to have them fringed around the outfield. Of course, they are after the players constantly, and can do it more conveniently at the easer range, but this verbal stuff has never bothered me much. They cannot distract my attention from the game because I do not answer them back, as a rule. If you show the crowd on the field you are not afraid of them, they won't upset or annoy you, and if some fellow does get your "goat," you have a chance to vent your spleen without yelling into the stand.

But the real reason why I like to have the crowd around the edge of the field, is because you can afford to take more chances on a fly ball. If there is one going over your head, you can jump for it and be sure of a soft place to land. Perhaps some readers might think this diving into the crowd dangerous, but I have never found it so. The individuals are considerate. It is only the gang spirit that makes it risky work. I have jumped into the crowd for many a fly ball and never received any bad treatment from it. As a rule, the fans will help even a visiting player up and pat him on the back if he has made a good play on the ball, saying:

"Good work, old man." Of if he has missed the ball: "Nice try, old boy." All you need do is to convince them you are not afraid. You would be surprised at the fairness of individuals in a crowd on the field.

Another phenomenon that I have discovered in my experience

with baseball crowds is that the loudest and most abusive "bugs" are the mildest and quietest off the field. Ball players, after they have been in the league awhile, unconsciously make a study of crowds and their habits. Generally, you will find that the fan who is always "riding" a player is a waiter or a bell hop or an elevator boy or some sort of servant who has no chance to assert himself except when he goes to a ball game. I don't mind having this sort yelling at me, and, as I have said, some of the best plays I ever made have been with the crowd fringing the field in critical games. It all adds to the tenseness of the atmosphere, which is most desirable. If I ever get into a world's series again, I would like to have the playing field entirely surrounded by a bunch of excitable, wild "nuts," but I am afraid this won't be the case, because there is a rule of National Commission now that no spectators are to be permitted on the diamond during the big series games.

Few fans know that the Athletics were mobbed in New York after one of the games in the 1913 world's series. It did not occur at the ball park, but in Seventh Avenue as their string of taxicabs was going from the Polo Grounds to the hotel. The team dressed at the hotel and went to and from the park in taxicabs, taking the Seventh Avenue route until the incident I have in mind occurred. "Eddie" Collins told me about it.

"'Strunkie' and 'Eddie' Murphy and I were riding down Seventh Avenue after the second game in New York when a bottle broke the window of our cab and showered glass all over us. The residents were evidently sore at our victory. Murphy was cut behind the ear, and the rest of us flopped down into the bottom of the cab while tomatoes, stones, bottles, and other missiles sizzled through our rig like sand through a sieve. The cops stood on the corners and laughed. After that, we went up Riverside Drive to 155th street for the games because we liked the looks of the residents along that route better."

II. The Effect of Crowds on Big Leaguers

This is a rare incident of modern baseball. Except during a world's series ball players do not now dress at the hotels but in the clubhouses at the parks. In the old days, however, the visiting teams almost always put on their uniforms in the hotels and went to the grounds in 'buses. This was in the days before the automobiles and taxicabs were plentiful, and those were the merry times. Only the home players had a clubhouse at the field then. After every close game, the visiting players were generally swarmed down upon by the crowd and had to fight their way clear or get police protection. Many a time, when I first broke into the league, I have left the field under police protection.

However, the change in the methods, which has resulted in the players dressing in the parks, has cut out most of these moving picture mob scenes. It is a strange thing that few fans will ever attack a player when he is in his street clothes, whereas they often will not hesitate to do so when he is in uniform. I have had wild "bugs" threaten to get me after the game because I have made some play or some kick, or perhaps because they thought I had tried to injure a player, only to find them waiting meek as lambs at the players' gate when I came out in my citizen's clothes. And instead of threatening or attacking me, they will yell:

"Hello, 'Ty'! How are you?"

I recall an incident that occurred one day when the Detroit club was in Cleveland. Olsen, who was playing third base on the Naps at that time, pushed me off the bag after I had slid in safe on a steal, and the umpire called me out. I had slid around the Cleveland third sacker with the hook and had my toe on the bag, being careful not to cut Olsen. When he shoved me off the bag, that got my "goat."

"Well, if that's the way you fellows are playing the game out here, I guess I'll have to come in a little differently after this when you are knocking runners off the bag after they are safe," I told Olsen.

Three or four innings later I got a double, and, although the Tigers had an easy lead and it was no stage to steal, I made up my mind to make a break for third on the first ball in order to show Olsen I was in earnest. I got my jump, the pitcher not expecting me to go at that stage, and slid into third "riding high" with spikes aglimmer, and making Olsen scurry for cover. The Cleveland third baseman had just caught the ball and my spikes in the air resulted in knocking it out of his hands toward the left field bleachers. I was on my feet in a moment and scored easily. The crowd let out a howl and threatened me with every dire thing it could think of because they thought I had intended to cut Olsen down. As far as the Cleveland player himself was concerned, he took the thing all right.

"Well, 'Ty,'" he said as he passed me on the way to the bench after the inning, "I guess we'll call the bet off."

"Sure," I replied.

But after that a deep voiced gink in the crowd right behind our bench, who reminded me of the boss bull frog in the pool, would croak at me every time there was a lull in the yelling or a kick on the decision:

"Dirty work! Dirty work, Cobb. I'll get you after the game! Look out for me at the players' gate after the game!"

This constant hammering at me in the silences of the contest got my "goat." I shouted something back in the man's general direction, and he bawled at me again. I couldn't see this fellow, but I was positive he must be big as a house, perhaps a "white hope" out for the afternoon. After the gate I went through the players' gate with three or four of the other boys.

"Hello, 'Ty.' How are you?" bellowed the same deep voice in friendly fashion. I looked for its owner and saw a strange phenomenon of nature, a man who reminded me of a tug boat with an ocean liner's whistle. He could not quite reach five feet in height.

"There's the guy," I told Moriarty, "who was going to eat me up after the game."

Yes, the crowd makes the game, and, I repeat, it seldom bothers me. But, of course, there is frequently the man in the stands with the big lungs and the constant repetition of a chant who is always bawling to you in the lulls, and he does get your "goat" once in a while.

One final word. The rhythmic cheering is most bothersome to pitchers, so they tell me. Veterans of the box say that the broken up shouting of the fans does not upset them any, but the constant hammering of one phrase wears on the nerves. "Nick" Altrock, the coacher with the Washington club, but formerly the great left-handed pitcher with the White Sox, used to be able to go to the coaching lines and, with one motion of his hand, get the spectators to cheer in beats. I believe these tactics won many a victory for the old White Sox.

The crowd certainly puts a man on edge and makes him play the game.

Chapter III

Sizing Up the Pitchers

Every Big League club develops a certain style of attack against the various pitchers. The aim is to shoot at the twirler's weakness. Every time a pitcher faces a batter, it is a game of wits. How the big batting stars size up certain twirlers. What sort of pitching the well-known hitters find hardest to bat. For instance "Home Run" Baker has great trouble in hitting Dubuc, of Detroit, because he is a slow ball pitcher. Secrets of the Big League stars.

"He hasn't got a thing but his glove, and that's got a hole in it. I'm off the 'movies' from here on. Every time I go to one of those film shows, it puts my eyes on the bum, and I can't hit the next day," I heard Frank Baker say after Dubuc, the little pitcher with the Detroit club, had struck him out one day in the summer of 1913.

Dubuc had been going good that afternoon. The Athletics had not been able to touch him. No matter how much the Detroit team may look like a dub outfit against other clubs, we always go well in our series with "Connie" Mack's crowd.

This is part of the peculiar psychology of baseball. In every league there is always some team, recognized by its standing to be weaker, that can consistently battle the strong to a finish. Brooklyn used to be able to win consistently from the old Cub machine when it was at its best and was cleaning up regularly on every other team in the National League. The Detroit team has always had difficulty in beating the Yankees, no matter how weak the New York American League club has been, and it has been very wobbly at times in the last few years. There is no particular reason for this paradox, except that perhaps the weaker club has won three or four games from the stronger some time before, and the idea is prevalent among the players on it that they can always win. This is the greatest tendency toward victory in anything, this idea that you have something on the other fellow.

But to return to Baker and his crack about Dubuc. That is one of the commonest remarks heard on a ball field when players are not batting. You will see a pitcher go through a game allowing three or four hits, and you will hear his victims in their clubhouse croaking afterwards:

"We certainly should have gotten to that guy out there to-day. He didn't have a thing on the ball."

A famous instance of this was the case of Richie, of the old Cubs, and his ability to beat the Giants. "Lew" could stand the New York team on its head any time he started against them for several reasons, yet frequently have I heard members of the Giants say:

"It's foolish we can't hit that bird. He has nothing, no fast one, no good curve, nothing but a little dinky out."

"Chief" Meyers was one of the worst complainers against Richie. It used to peeve the "Chief" badly to get up there with his big bat and hope in his heart that he would knock that tantalizing slow one of Richie's out of the lot, only to miss three. Meyers was talking to me about it one day during the 1912 world's series, and his plaints were pitiful to hear.

"It makes me rave," remarked the "Chief," "to think that I can't reach that fellow Richie. He hasn't got anything. I'll bet the next time we get a crack at him he dives for the shower-bath about the third inning, and will be glad to get there."

That is another familiar phrase of ball players. They are always going to drive the easy pitcher who keeps beating them, to the shower bath the next time they get a crack at him.

"We only hope he starts against us again in this series," they boast. "We'll show him up for what he is."

But he starts again, and they don't show him up. He has something on them. This is true of Dubuc and the Athletics, and especially Baker. Other clubs hit Dubuc, but the Athletics seldom do. And yet they all say he "hasn't got a thing." It makes Baker particularly sore, as I honestly believe Dubuc is the hardest pitcher in the league for the great third baseman of Philadelphia to hit, and Frank certainly likes his batting average. He can't connect with Dubuc's slow ball, which is an excellent product. Baker maintains that moving picture shows hurt his eyes, although some players call them "eye tonic." I think Baker always takes one in the night before he expects Dubuc to work, so as to be sure of his alibi.

"No more movies," repeats "Bake" after a bad day. "A ball player must be crazy to take chances like that with his eyes."

On the other hand, if a club is hitting a pitcher, the players will say he has everything, but that they are enjoying a good day at bat. Take, for instance, the case of Marquard in that first game of the world's series in 1913. Of course, there is the personal angle to this. If a pitcher has a lot of stuff, and the batters are banging him, it is all the more to their credit.

Clarke Griffith is a great man to "ride" his players to keep them from getting puffed up over their ability and to keep them away from the prima donna class and notions. We were playing a game with the Washington club one day last summer, and the Senators were slamming a young pitcher we had working all over the field.

"That kid hasn't got much," I heard Griffith say to one of his players during the contest. "It's pretty soft for you hitters. You can fatten up your batting averages out there to-day, and they all need it."

"Hasn't got much?" replied the player in question. "I wish you would get out there and take a look at his stuff. His curve has a hook on it like a hairpin, and you can hardly see his fast one. We've just got our eyes with us to-day. That's all."

The player in question had already made three hits.

"That's old bunk," returned Griffith. "Whenever you guys are hitting, the pitcher always has lots of stuff. I wish there was a fellow out there every day with a hook like a hairpin on his curve and a good fast one if that gink has all this stuff."

When Marquard opened the 1913 world's series for the Giants, he was very nervous and seemed to discard all his pitching knowledge after he had entered the box. He warmed up in such excellent style that McGraw made up his mind at the last minute to take a chance on him in the opening game. "Rube" is naturally very nervous under a strain, so all the players who know anything about him tell me. "Billy" Evans knew him when he played in Indianapolis and lived in Cleveland, and he says the same thing. The strain that day was a big one, as it always is in the opening game of a world's series, or any game, for that matter. Marquard did not try to work the batters in that first game as he had been coached to do, and the wiser heads on the Athletics, who know baseball, told me afterwards that they did not see he carried any stuff at all.

"Never saw a pitcher look so bad," one of the Philadelphia veterans told me. "There was no hop on his fast one, and we never saw a curve ball while Marquard was in the game."

But the younger players on the Athletics, who fattened up their averages and made a good showing on Marquard's pitching that day, did not turn in the same testimony.

"How did Marquard look out there to-day?" I asked one of them after the contest. "He didn't have much, did he?"

"Yes, he did," was the reply. "He had a lot of stuff. He looked pretty good out there to-day."

"What would you do to him if you ever caught him on an off day, then?" I inquired.

"Well, 'Ty,'" he answered, "you've got to remember that our club has a lot of hard hitters on it."

McGraw employs methods similar to those of Griffith to discourage players from believing they are wonderful stickers, if they happen to have one good day. He does this only in the cases of men who lack ambition and feel that three or four hits in one afternoon mean that they can lie back and take it easy for two or three days afterwards.

They tell a story about the way he used to ride "Josh" Devore, the former left fielder. "Josh" was a good money player, a man who could rise to meet the occasion when a critical situation presented itself. It will be recalled by the regular fans how he saved one game for the Giants in the 1912 world's series by a remarkable catch off Nunamaker in the last inning. But "Josh," they say, was a little shy on ambition during the regular season. If Devore should get a long hit, a three-bagger for instance, and slide into third thinking pretty well of himself, McGraw in the coaching box would be there with this remark:

"I guess that bird in there hasn't got much on the ball to-day when even you can whang him that way. How do you hit them when you shut your eyes?"

This would incline Devore, who made nearly as much mileage last season shifting from one team in the National League to another, as the world's tourists did on their trip around the world, to the belief that he would have to keep hustling to hold his job. That is just what McGraw wanted.

III. Sizing Up the Pitchers

While we are on the subject of Devore and pitchers, I would like to relate a little incident which occurred during the 1911 world's series between the Giants and the Athletics. It will be remembered that the New York club took the first game played at the Polo Grounds on Saturday, and on Monday morning the Giants were on their way over to Philadelphia in a special car reserved for the ball players. As I was writing the stories of the contests for the newspapers, I was travelling in the same train, and the ball players and newspaper reporters were all together in the special car. Finally, a newspaper man, who is a very good friend of mine, brought Devore up and introduced him to me.

"I'm glad to meet you, 'Ty,'" he said. "I want to sit down and talk to you."

"Suppose you have heard a lot about me and all that regular stuff," said I, kidding. "Sit down."

He planted himself in the seat beside me and began to talk baseball, finally switching around to American League pitchers and then narrowing the discussion down to the twirling staff of the Athletics. At last, he devoted all his attentions to Plank. He asked me question after question about "Eddie" and his pitching weaknesses. Of course, because I was a loyal American Leaguer, I filled him full of misinformation, seeing what he was driving at.

"What's this guy's greatest weakness?" inquired the ingenuous "Josh."

"Wait for his cross fire," I solemnly told him. "That has been greatly overrated. It's a cinch to hit." Plank's cross fire, when right, is almost unhittable.

"Once we get on the bases with him working, we'll win," suggested "Josh." "If he doesn't cut his motion down, we'll run wild on him, and no left handers are as strong without the motion. How about this bird?"

"Don't take too many chances when you are on first base," I even more solemnly told him. "He's got a great motion to the bag and can hold runners close."

Now, that is Plank's greatest weakness. He has a bad move toward first base, and is one of the few pitchers with a bad motion to hold runners near the bag who has been really great. This is well known in the American League. So "Josh" and I talked on until we reached the Broad Street station, or, rather, I talked and "Josh" did most of the listening. Finally, he said good-bye and left me. I have been told since that he was greatly encouraged by his conversation with me. Said he to another member of the New York club as they were getting off the train:

"Met Cobb on the way over this morning, and he is a great fellow. And I pumped him about Plank's weaknesses. Got a lot of information. They say I can't hit left handers, hey [a notable and recognized batting weakness of Devore's]? Well, I just hope they start Plank against us this afternoon."

Plank did start, and "Josh" did not get even a foul off his delivery, if my memory serves me right. He could not touch Plank. Since then, I have felt rather sorry for Devore being shuttled around from one club to another. He is a very likable fellow and has played a lot of good ball, especially in important series. I considered him to be one of the big stars of the contests between the Giants and the Red Sox in 1912. But I had to laugh for myself when he was shifted from Cincinnati to Philadelphia in the latter part of the 1913 season, and announced that he would then tell the Phillies how to beat the Giants out and win the pennant from his old teammates. He was about as successful in this as he was in hitting Plank.

This rather lengthy introduction, into which I have injected incidents, has had for its purpose to show that it is hard to say which pitcher is the best in the Big Leagues. One man is invincible against certain clubs and easy for others. He looks good on certain days and under certain circumstances. I am speaking now of the twirlers rated as stars of the game. It is a case of psychology. Probably a team has hit one man hard the first day, or maybe the first two or three times he faced them, and they have accumulated the idea that they can always hit him, and they do. He also gets the same idea, and he has not much stuff because all he is waiting for is the signal from the bench for him to get out of the box. I think I mentioned in a previous story the case of "Jim" Scott, of the White Sox, who has always been able to beat the Athletics with great frequency because the first time he worked against them he pitched them to death. He has believed ever since that he has something on them, and so do they. He cannot tell anyone else how he does it.

Then there is "Ed" Walsh. For a long time "Connie" Mack's team knew when Walsh was going to pitch the spitball by an unconscious move he made with his eyebrows, if he really wet the ball, that caused the peak of his cap to vacillate up and down. If he was bluffing, the peak did not move. They would hammer Walsh when they knew what was coming, because he uses little besides the spitter and his fast one, and, having acquired the belief they could beat him, they still hit him hard, although not as consistently, even after "Ed" had been tipped off to the fact that he made this unconscious move and had covered it up.

Matty has been able to win from the Cincinnati club with great frequency because, the story is, he took two or three games in a row, years ago, and he got to believe he always would win, and so did the Reds. They say the first game of the long series of victories that Mathewson hung up against the Reds was won when Matty was pitching his head off because he got sore at some remark Clarke Griffith, then the Cincinnati manager, had made to him from the coacher's box. Often a little thing like that will have a lasting influence. The last thing in the world which will worry Matty, or, in fact, any seasoned veterans, is "kidding" from the coaching box. But Mathewson was young when Griffith tried it, and the "old fox" did not know what a boomerang his joshing was going to turn out to be. Matty always had trouble winning from the Cubs of old. So it goes.

Frequently, there is one individual batter who can hit some one pitcher hard, even though he may be weak against other twirlers of far less ability. It is because the man believes he has something on this twirler. Take the case of Tinker and Mathewson. They say the old Cub shortstop beat the New York star out of more games than any one player in baseball. On the other hand, Wagner could never hit "Bugs" Raymond as well as he could other pitchers, because Raymond kidded the great Pittsburgh shortstop from the box and it got his German goat, to think his dignity should be reflected upon. Therefore, it is hard to rate pitchers and say which one is the best. A man is good against one club and weak against another, or strong against some batters and putty for others.

However, there is one pitcher I would rate above all others. Right off hand, I do not think of a single club against which he is weak or a single Big League batter, in fact. Of course, some men hit him harder than others, but this can be laid more to the individual ability of the batters than to the idea that they have anything on him. The pitcher I refer to is Walter Johnson, of the Washington team, and I consider him the greatest in the world.

He combines everything that a successful twirler needs. He has a fine, fast breaking curve, and he is famous for his speed. I do not exaggerate when I say that his fast one has been so good on a dark day that I have never seen the ball pass me and am only aware of the fact because I have heard it strike the catcher's glove. He also has the smooth, even, unexcitable temperament found in all the best pitchers. Nothing worries or irritates him. He is afraid of no team or no hitter. He knows he has the stuff, and he goes into the box to win. His opponents make little difference to him. Johnson also has very sound sense.

Like most young pitchers, when he first came to the Washington club, he was eager to make a great record and sensational start for himself, and he knew he had the stuff. He used to put all he had on every ball he pitched, and would go through the games right along with the hits against him totaling less than five. His players behind him got to figuring that one run was enough to win for them with Johnson pitching and, with this margin, they would quit hustling for runs. Pitchers on opposing teams would duck the assignment to go into the box against the Washington wonder, pleading a sore arm or some other alibi, but really foreseeing defeat—a condition which helped to beat them before they started—and not being anxious to have an almost positive cavity put into their records without even the chance of a run for their money. Even now, when a pitcher beats Johnson it is hard to convince him that he is not the wonder of the world.

But Johnson has changed his tactics recently and is saving himself. He is ambitious to last a record length of time at his chosen profession and continue to draw down his record salary for some years to come. A few seasons ago, he rousted some of the players for not hustling harder to get runs behind him when he was in the box. He was talking to me about this one day last summer.

"I used to hand them everything I carried all the time, no matter what the situation was," he told me. "But, taking a tip from Griffith and otherwise pitchers like Bender, Mathewson, and Plank, I have laid off giving them both barrels at all stages. If I have a comfortable lead, I slow up. They make runs for the other twirlers, why shouldn't they for me?"

When he slows up, he is better than most of them at top speed. There has been a lot of talk about the Athletics stealing battery signs, and I will have more to say about this in a subsequent article, but if they want to get signs against Johnson and take a chance, they are welcome to the information. I would not take signs against him if they offered me double the salary I get for doing it. What good would the money do me if I was only fit for the undertaker? I don't want to be tipped off to a curve and be up there set for it, only to be greeted by a fast one, from which there is no opportunity to get away with Johnson throwing the ball. I'd hate to have him "bean" me.

Of course, I have never batted against Mathewson, but I have seen him pitch frequently, and he is one grand performer. In the last two world's series, he gave some wonderful exhibitions of pitching and nerve, with his team crumbling and throwing him down behind him. He has had things go against him in such a way that the nerve of ninety-nine per cent, of the Big League pitchers would have been broken under the same circumstances. But he keeps right on working.

The exhibition he gave in the 1913 world's series, while pitching against Plank in the second game in Philadelphia, was nothing short of marvelous, and probably the best single piece of pitching I have ever seen. With three men on the bases, and none out in the last half of the ninth, and with just one run needed by the Athletics to win, he kept the plate clean. Mind you, he did that with his team nervous, shaken, and practically conceding defeat behind him, and having no evident faith in his supporters, himself. It is my opinion that if those balls which retired two runners at the plate had been hit to any other infielder than the veteran Wiltse, who was playing first base as a substitute that day, the Athletics would have won the series in four straight games, because all the rest of McGraw's infielders were up in the air at the time. Matty is probably the greatest money pitcher that ever lived, but Johnson is the greatest pitcher of them all to-day without any qualifications to his title of king.

Most successful pitchers have a good move toward first base to hold up runners, because, if your opponents are going to run wild on the bases, a pitcher will have a tough time winning ball games. As I have said, there is only one big star in the American League who has been a real success without this carefully developed move. This is "Eddie" Plank, and he covers up his weakness well, and the natural strength of the Athletics also helps him to conceal it. He is a left hander, of course, and faces first before he pitches so he can watch the baserunner. Very few men, therefore, risk a long lead in spite of his awkward throw to the bag.

Many pitchers have spent years developing a good move toward first base to hold up runners, and this one thing has kept several men in fast company after they did not have much else left. Walsh, Mathewson, Bender, Rucker, nearly all the stars, in fact, have good moves to first. "Ed" Walsh has one of the best in the American League, a move that has nipped many a runner and is so near a balk that players have frequently urged umpires to call it on him. Walsh will raise his shoulder slightly, an action that in most men is a sure sign they are going to deliver the ball to the batter, and then he swings and drives it to first base. It has caught many a runner flat footed. And the peculiar thing about it is that this move would not get a poor base runner who does not have sense enough to look for the little things. Walsh grabs off the best base runners in his league right along, in spite of the fact that his efficiency in this specialty is universally known. The stars, wise in their profession, do not tip off a base runner when they are going to pitch, because the smart player is always looking for some little sign made unconsciously.

A good many pitchers have a knee move. Frank Smith, formerly of the White Sox, always looked toward third base when he was going to throw to first with a runner on. Any time he looked at the catcher, it was a safe bet he would not throw over again, and a runner could get his start.

Many pitchers with the really great moves are to be found in the minors, because they have not the stuff to accompany this excellent accomplishment. "Bill" Burns, formerly with the Cincinnati Nationals and now with the Minneapolis team of the American Association; "Billy" Campbell, a southpaw with Mobile, and Walter Slagle, all have great moves to first that are half balks, but which are not pronounced enough to be called. These left handers apparently start to pitch and then shoot the ball to first base. That old story is told about all of them of the busher at the bat who struck at a ball when it was thrown to first base, he being so entirely taken in by the balk notion.

They say that Drucke, once with the Giants, who started out with the prospects of being a good pitcher but who fell down, had an unconscious move with his knee which cost him many a game. Of course, after a base runner discovers some slight move in a pitcher that tips him off when the box artist is going to pitch, he tries to keep his knowledge a secret except for the members of his own team. Managers, and the pitchers themselves, are always watching for some move that is tipping base runners off. McGraw finally broke Drucke of this bad habit, but they say he felt uncomfortable without it, and that it hurt his pitching.

The old type of coaching, the abusive and kidding sort that was intended to worry a pitcher, has largely passed out of baseball except in the case of an occasional youngster who may be worried by it. Matty was telling me after the game he won in the 1913 world's series that some of the younger players on the bench were trying to worry Plank by yelling at him such things as:—"What are you doing out there pitching—an old man like you?"

"I jumped on these fellows," said Matty. "'Don't try that on an old bird like Plank,' I told them. 'You might go after some young fellow, but he eats that stuff.'"

As I have said, it is hard to rate pitchers. "Tom" Hughes could throw his glove into the box and beat Cleveland nearly any time when he was in the league, while all the rest of the clubs would generally wallop him. Plank has ever been effective against Detroit. The Tigers have always believed a southpaw hard for them to beat. Matty is almost sure to win from Cincinnati, and so on. The old superstitions and traditions stick, in spite of the fact that the players on the various clubs are changed here and there every season. But there is one bird who is good against all of them, and his name is Walter Johnson. My hope is to watch him in a world's series some time before he begins to wear out. I don't think there would be any series. He could pitch every day if necessary. He is the greatest pitcher alive.

♦ Chapter IV ♦

Inside Stuff
About the "Umps"

In some ways, the umpires are the bravest men in baseball, for they all face tough situations in their careers. In this story, I have related some thrilling exhibitions of nerve that certain arbiters have displayed. Also there is brilliant repartee between umpires and players in nearly every game, and the anecdotes in this story include snatches of these word passes. It is an insight into the character of the umpires as I know them. Also humorous occurrences.

Most fans think my umpire reputation is a bad one. The general impression is that an umpire has as soothing an effect on me as a red rag has on the temper or temperament of a peevish bull. This is altogether wrong, as I will endeavor to show. It may be true that I was a little rough on umpires when I first broke into the Big League, but I have long since seen the folly of this course. The bad name has stuck to me, however. It is customary to keep after umpires in the bush leagues, and I tried to maintain my pace when I came up. That's how I made my mistake.

Now listen to the way I really feel toward the umpires. After I had been in the league for a time, I met some of the umpires off the

"You're the umpire," replied the nurse.

field and found that they were human and pretty good fellows. I prize my friendships with several umpires now as highly as any I have. Lately I have made it my business not to show up an umpire by violent gestures at him on the field, so that the crowd can "hop" on him. If I think a man has missed one on me, I will walk by him and tell him quietly that I believe he has made a mistake, but I never try to get the crowd down on an arbiter any more.

"Billy" Evans has made me the hero of several of his umpire stories, and Evans and I are good friends. If he is going to do this, I don't see why I should not turn around and make him the leading man in some of mine. But the first umpire incident which comes to my mind is connected with that grand old battler, "Tim" Hurst, now out of the majors. "Tim" had many stormy sessions while umpiring, and the history of the game is full of the battles of Hurst.

When the subway was first put into New York, many out-of-town folks were confused by the Broadway and Bronx trains. Frequently passengers would get on a Bronx express and forget to change at Ninety-sixth street, so that instead of arriving at the old American League Park they found themselves in the Bronx Zoo, or somewhere along this route. This would make a difference of about an hour in the time of arrival at the ball park. I would not call this a plain, bonehead play, because I made the same mistake myself, once.

"Tim" was scheduled to work a game out at American League Park when the Detroit club was playing there one day, and he got carried up into the Bronx instead of going on the right route. Hurst has told me since that he was reading some promising prize fighter's history at the time and paid no attention to the stations. Nobody was scheduled to help Hurst umpire this game, so that when the time for the contest arrived and "Tim" had not shown up, we were up against it for an umpire. Griffith, then managing the Yankees, sent for Jennings, and they held a confab at the plate while the players of both clubs gathered around.

"I'll tell you what I'll do," said "Foxy" Griffith. "One of my extra players will work behind the bat, and you can put one of your men on the bases." The rule book provides for substitute players to umpire in the event of an emergency.

"All right," replied Jennings, and selected an extra player from the bench in whom he had confidence to see things right and call them as he saw them.

"Germany" Schaefer was playing second base on the Detroit club in those days, and he smashed the ball to right field in the first inning.

It was really a single, but "Germany," figuring that he wasn't going to get any the worst of it from a player of his own club umpiring on the bases if there was a close play at second, decided to take two on the punch. The play at second base was close, Schaefer being forced to slide for it, but our volunteer umpire was properly on the job and shouted:

"Safe!"

"Germany" was up and brushing himself off, being rather tickled with the fact that he had made a two base hit, when he heard a deep, contradictory voice break out behind him:

"Yer out!"

"Germany" looked and saw Hurst right behind him. He had come hustling across the field when he saw the hit and had got close enough to second base to take the play there. None of the rest of us had noticed him. Schaefer put up an awful kick and bawled Hurst out, but "Tim" bawled back and stuck to his decision.

"You were late, and you are incompetent," declared Schaefer. "If you would keep away from the race tracks, you might be on the job. How do you expect to call them from the clubhouse?"

"You don't make the plays close enough for me to need to be any nearer to see them," replied Hurst, who was always there with the come-back. "Now get out of there and go to the bench before I put you out of the game."

Hurst was umpiring in Detroit one day, when we were playing the Athletics, and he called "Danny" Murphy safe at first base on a slow roller down the third base line, which Moriarty steamed across the diamond ahead of the runner. At least I thought he did from where I was standing in right field. I was playing close behind first base, and Murphy seemed to be out a step. Hurst called him safe, however, which got my "goat."

"He was out a yard, 'Tim,'" I yelled, running in to where Hurst was standing back of first.

The umpire paid no attention to me, and I finally went back to right field. Pretty soon another batter pushed one to the second baseman and was thrown out before he was much more than half way down the line. I was still sore about the other decision and thought I would cut loose with a little sarcasm.

"How about that, 'Tim'? He was safe, too, I suppose," I yelled as I ran in to the umpire.

"Well," said "Tim," "is that what you think?"

"Sure," I answered, still holding my ground.

"All right, I'll call him that way if you want it. Now which was he?"

"He was out," I was forced to admit, because I knew "Tim" would have reversed his decision and called him safe if I had continued to say he was. That was always "Tim's" style.

"Rube" Oldring, of the Athletics, tells a story on Hurst when "Rube" first broke into the league. "Tim" was working behind the bat one day, and he called a strike on Oldring that looked bad to the Philadelphia outfielder, or that he wanted the crowd, for he was playing at home, to think looked bad to him.

"That wasn't a strike," said Oldring.

"Strike one, I said," replied "Tim."

Pretty soon up came the next pitch.

"Ball one," decided Hurst.

"Right where the other one was, 'Tim,'" declared Oldring, thinking to prove in this way that Hurst had missed the first one.

"All right," said Hurst. "Strike two."

"What?" shouted Oldring.

"That's what you said, yourself," returned "Tim." "You thought it was right where the first one was."

And Hurst made it stick, too. Oldring lost a strike and put himself in a hole through his kick.

But the old time umpires of the rough and ready Hurst school are fast passing out of the game. I cannot think of one of his style in the Big League now. If a catcher kicked with "Tim" working and tried to bark Hurst's shins with his spikes, Timothy would kick right back at the catcher's shins while he argued and generally tore off as much epidermis, because the catchers of his day did not wear shin guards as a general rule.

There is one thing that ball players are forced to admire in umpires and that is nerve. No man lasts long in the Big Leagues as an umpire without this quality. Big Leaguers make it their business to test out the nerve of umpires at once as soon as they break in, so that there will never be any question in the minds of the players as to whether they are "yellow" or not. If either a ball player or an umpire comes into the Big League and displays any lack of nerve, he might just as well pack his grip and pull out again. There is no room for him.

There is an interesting story of how "Billy" Evans happened to go to work as an umpire. He was a newspaper reporter in Youngstown, Ohio, after he left Cornell University. He had been quite a student up there as I get it, having played football until he hurt his knee, and having sung in the glee club, I think. When he got back to Youngstown, he had all the "rah rah" trimmings and was a good dresser off and on and popular with the Youngstown society buds. But the newspaper business was not very remunerative in the small town.

Evans was doing baseball, covering the bush league games in the local lot, when the club was short an umpire one day. Evans had shown considerable baseball intelligence in that neighborhood, so they asked him if he would crash out of the press stand and into the gap and umpire the game. They offered him $5 for the afternoon's work, which looked like a lot of money considering that his weekly pay envelope at the newspaper office only carried $12. "Billy" figured he was making about half of his salary in one afternoon in this way, and it looked pretty soft until he had gone through one game. They tell me that was a tough town to umpire in.

However, he supplied so much general satisfaction to both parties by his umpiring on the first day that they asked him to work all the games played in town, and gave him a flat price of $5 per battle. "Billy" says his hardest work was on Sundays, when the real sporting element of the town, confined to the shops and other industries through the week, turned out to root, and incidentally considered mobbing the umpire as one of their privileges. Of course, as soon as it became locally known among the society buds that Evans was umpiring on Sundays, his social rating slumped, but his financial standing took a big jump, and "Bill" has ever preferred the financial position to the social one. He kept on with the newspaper, writing the story of the game each day after he had finished his work as an umpire.

"Jimmy" McAleer, the great outfielder who played with Cleveland and who has since managed the St. Louis and Washington clubs and was the president of the Boston Red Sox, lived in Youngstown, and he stopped there one Sunday when his club had an off day to see his folks. He took advantage of the opportunity to go down and watch the bushers play, thinking perhaps he might see one to his liking who would help his club. Anyway, you cannot keep a baseball man from a ball game, no matter how strongly they insist that they wish the National Commission would pass a by-law barring them from all ball parks. McAleer made no progress in his search for budding talent, but he was impressed by the way in which Evans handled the contest, the young colleger getting away with a lot of tough situations.

At this time Ban Johnson was shy on umpires for the American League, and he mentioned the fact to "Jimmy" McAleer one day.

"There's a young fellow down in Youngstown getting away with the Sunday games in good shape," said McAleer. "Name is Evans. That's a tough town to work in, because they take their pleasure mobbing umpires."

"I'll have a look at him," said Mr. Johnson.

The president of the American League sent for Evans and offered him a trial, but "Billy" did not accept at once.

"I want to put it up to my mother," replied Evans.

His mother finally consented after Evans proved to her that the prospects of an umpire in the Big League were much brighter financially than those of a newspaper reporter in Youngstown, Ohio. His employer on the newspaper told him that he could have his old job back if he failed to give satisfaction in the Big League, so Evans went to Chicago and worked his first game there. He still wore his good clothes and had the college-boy air, which riled some of the old-timers on the White Sox, such as "Jiggs" Donohue, who afterwards went crazy, and two or three others. Of course, all the ball players were "riding" Evans in the first game to try out his nerve, and he had some tough ones to call. One was against Donohue.

"I'll get you for that one," proclaimed "Jiggs" in loud tones so all the other ball players could hear him. "I'll beat your head off."

"You're welcome to," replied Evans. "I'll be in my room in the Great Northern Hotel at eight o'clock to-night if you can come around and do the job. For the present, do your beating to the club-house."

Donohue never showed to keep the date with Evans. Even after this, however, Evans had a lot of rough traveling to do, the Big League dazzling him a good deal and each new batch of ball players being after him. That was the day of the old-school ball player, and they could not understand Evans' style and his neat manner. They were more used to the "Tim" Hurst sort.

"Billy" got the name of being the worst umpire in the league until he went to work in a game in St. Louis one Sunday. Now, St. Louis is no peace-loving burg when it sees an umpire, for in that town an umpire must assimilate the blame and a lot of cushions, bottles, etc., for all evils. Evans had so tough a battle to go through that the management decided that it was best for purposes of personal safety to call the police before they permitted him to depart from the field. He was leaving, protected in this way, when some fan shied a bottle at long range and it hit Evans right behind the ear.

For a time it was thought that the umpire was dead. They carted him off to the hospital, although most of those present had an idea that his destination should have been the morgue. He did not come to until late in the night, when the nurse read some extras to him about how an umpire had been killed at the ball park that day.

"Who was he?" said Evans.

"You're the umpire," replied the nurse.

"So I'm the dead one, am I?" asked Evans. "Well, I guess I'll show them yet whether they got me or not."

The physicians themselves were not so sure of the future, but Evans eventually got better and went back to umpiring with just as much nerve as ever he had. By this time he had won the respect of all the players, and he has been one of the best umpires in the business ever since. He is unbiased in his decisions.

Evans and I have had several jams over plays. He tells the story of how I put one over on him in Detroit one day when I had an engagement to go to an early dinner in the country club outside of town. The Tigers had cinched the pennant late in the season of 1909, and the game was an unimportant one and could make no difference to my club. It dragged out to an hour and a half, and only six innings had been completed. I saw I would never be able to keep my dinner engagement unless I got put out of the game. I began to kick on every play, but Evans, being in a good humor, refused to get sore. Finally I came to bat in the seventh inning. One cut the plate.

"Strike!" said Evans.

I tossed my hat and bat into the air and held my hands a yard apart to show him how bad and how much off the plate I considered the ball to be. This was an unpardonable sin, as I was showing the umpire up before the crowd, something none of the "umps" will stand for.

"What's the matter, 'Ty'?" asked Evans. "That was a good ball. What are you trying to show me up for?"

"That one was a yard off the plate," I said, and again I stretched out my hands to show him.

"Get out of the game and beat it," replied Evans.

I hurled my bat at the pile in front of the bench and sprinted for the clubhouse. Schaefer, who had been coaching at first base, came in toward the plate when I made my kick and heard it all. As soon as I had been put out of the game, he said to Evans:

"That's just what Cobb wanted. He had a dinner date and was afraid of being late."

By this time I had reached second base in my hurried journey to the clubhouse.

"Come back here and get into the game," bawled Evans after me.

But I could not hear him, in fact did not want to, and just kept right on going. I kept my engagement. The next day the umpire said to me:

"Got any early dates for this afternoon, 'Ty'? Because, if you have, cancel them. You could not blow yourself out of this game to-day with a freight car full of nitroglycerine."

"No, I'll play until dark if you say so," I replied, "but I'm much obliged to you for letting me off early yesterday."

I got into a more serious jam with Evans earlier in my baseball days. I had not been hitting well for a week and was sore and peevish over it. At that time I would permit my temper to flare up instanter, and I would say things that I did not mean. Twice I had gone to the bat that day and had failed to hit safe. The third time Evans called a strike on me that looked low, and I thought he was putting me in the hole and hurting my average. I threw down my bat and began to bark at him. He paid no attention, but got the whiskbroom and began to clean off the plate. Still I talked. I threw my cap into the air, and when he had finally completed the job of cleaning the plate he looked at me again. He could not miss the actions, for I was still kicking in pantomime.

"Get out of the game," he said.

"I'll knock your block off for this," I challenged, having lost all sense by now.

"Not here, 'Ty,'" replied Evans, who has great control over his temper, as an umpire must. "But come around to my dressing-room after the game and we'll settle it."

After my shower, I cooled off and was sorry for what I had said. As soon as the game was over I hurried around to the umpire's dressing-room to square it with Evans.

"Hello, 'Ty'!" he said. "Did you call to battle?"

"I will if you want me to," I replied, "but what are you always picking on me for, Bill? I'm sorry I talked and acted the way I did out there to-day, but you called a bad one on me."

"We all of us boot one once in awhile," replied Evans, and that was the end of it.

The gamest piece of umpiring I ever saw pulled off on a ball field was in the seventeen-inning contest between Detroit and Philadelphia in 1907, which ended in a tie and really gave Detroit the pennant. Philadelphia fans have never got over the decision of

"Silk" O'Loughlin on that occasion, and both the Tigers and the umpire are still bitterly hated in that town for no other reason, I believe.

Because of the importance of the contest and the closeness of the pennant fight, all were under a terrific strain—players, umpires, and spectators. The men on both clubs had been fighting neck and neck and were "crabbing" all the way, finding fault with fellow-players who, it was thought, had committed some sin which had been costly to their chances. But I will have more to say about the feelings of the players at that time in a subsequent article.

Around the outfield was a crowd restrained by ropes, and there was a ground rule that a hit into the crowd would go for two bases. With the score tied in the seventeenth inning and the Athletics, the home team, at bat, and with a man on base, the ball was hit toward Crawford. Sam went back for the ball, which was near the edge of the crowd, and right alongside of a policeman stationed inside of the ropes. This policeman, whose name I do not know—in fact, I never have heard as far as I can recall—forgot for a minute that he was working for the Philadelphia police force and not the Philadelphia ball club. Crawford was back set for the catch when the policeman bobbed up and was hit by the ball. Of course, it rolled into the crowd for what looked like two bases, and the Athletics apparently had the battle won. Connolly was umpiring on the bases, and he called the man safe, declaring the hit to be all right.

The whole Detroit team swarmed around O'Loughlin, the head umpire, for a decision, urging that the ball had been interfered with. The crowd was already shouting over the victory. "Silk" called Connolly, the umpire on the bases, in to the plate. By this time some of the fans had climbed on to the field and were making threatening gestures at O'Loughlin and the Detroit players. The strain was telling and the storm about to break.

"Did the cop interfere, 'Tommy'?" asked O'Loughlin.

"Yes," answered Connolly.

"The batter's out, then," said O'Loughlin.

The crowd charged, but "Silk" held his ground until the police took him off to safety. That piece of nervy umpiring gave the Detroit club a pennant, for the game ended in a tie, and we finally won the championship by the slenderest of margins. It was rare gameness to find in any man, and the finest piece of work I ever saw on a ball field.

Most umpires are like prima donnas. Nearly every one has some groove. "Billy" Evans is the best dresser in our league, "Silk" O'Loughlin has the best voice and admits it, "Jack" Egan carries the keenest wit and whets it on us ball players, and so on. They tell me that "Bill" Klem is the czar of the National League. He worked in the world's series that was played between Detroit and Pittsburgh back in 1909. He seemed to be a good, square umpire, as, in fact, they all are.

The best umpires are the ones who are smart, because they are the superior judges of human nature, and half of the battle of the profession is in studying the temperament of players. The sort of handling which will fit one type of player will rub another one the wrong way all the time. Big bruisers are not good umpires, though the best recommendation an official of the old days could get was: "He licked somebody in the Three I League. He ought to do."

The demand now is for the umpire who knows men and knows baseball and a man who is reasonable, and not for pugilists. The improvement in the type of umpires has kept pace with the improvement in the class of ball players during recent years.

Nobody can or ever does conclude a story on umpires without one last fling at "Tim" Hurst. Years ago, "Cap" Anson was touring the country with a show called the "Runaway Colt." In it was a baseball scene which called for an umpire. In the various cities where the production was put on some baseball celebrity was selected to act as the umpire in this scene. When it came to New York they, of course, dug up "Tim." "Arlie" Latham was the man in the show who did the slide for a base in this scene. He did it with all the realism characteristic of a Belasco production. Hurst, getting into the spirit of the thing, was down over the play.

"Yer out!" shouted "Tim," jerking his thumb over his shoulder.

Latham, always strong for the dramatic, desired to add an extra touch. He jumped up to kick and, as he straightened with a quick motion, his head bumped "Tim" in the nose and started it bleeding. Hurst swung on "Arlie" and floored him. The crowd went crazy and demanded the same scene each night, which Hurst and "Arlie" refused to supply.

Well, now that the umpires know what I think of them, I hope that they will improve their opinion of me next season, although they don't miss many for me. After all, as a rule, it is only a difference of one word that makes all the trouble for the umpires. Sometimes they say "Out" when several ball players think it should have been "Safe." "Silk" O'Loughlin denies this. He says there is no such thing as a questionable decision in baseball, that a man is either out or safe; and "Silk" admits that he always knows which when he is working.

◆ CHAPTER V ◆

Big League Bosses
and Their Methods

*This is the real story of how the celebrated managers of baseball
work during a hard contest, with incidents illustrating how they
have applied their knowledge of the game in a pinch. In every contest in the Big League, there comes a break when the changing of a
pitcher or the substitution of a batter may mean victory or defeat, a
championship or second place. Managers must face these situations
and decide in a moment what to do. How the various leaders do their
work and handle the temperamental stars on their clubs.*

Good managers are like black pearls, or hens' teeth, or any of
those things which are quoted as being so scarce. Big League leaders are judged by the results they obtain, and it is their methods
which bring the results, since, notwithstanding that the players on
the clubs change year after year, you usually find the same managers
up fighting for the pennant.

Money does not make successful managers, as "Connie" Mack
has proven. He looks at the date on a nickel seven or eight times
before he spends it for a player, and yet he has the most valuable collection ever assembled under one standard. The only time "Connie"

"Jennings is a hurrah fellow, with everything out in front."

ever did cut loose and spend money for a ball player his results were practically a net loss. I refer to the time he paid $12,000 for "Lefty" Russell and then had to turn him back to the minor leagues.

Fans who live in a town where a team is a consistent loser generally insist that it is a shame for the management not to go out and buy stars and put a winner into their city. They imagine that any club, willing to spend the money, can take a pennant.

"Look at 'Connie' Mack," I have heard followers of baseball remark. "He has the stars. Why don't the St. Louis Browns buy some of this players? Mack must spend money to get them."

But "Connie" does not spend the money. He gathers in his players through a carefully developed method, and he would not sell a single finished product for a sum that would amount to a fortune. After Brooklyn had paid $25,000 for "Joe" Tinker, Mack announced that he would not sell "Eddie" Collins for $100,000. Perhaps that was a plank in a new publicity platform of Mack's which has resulted from recent suggestions of the Philadelphia club owners. These are not to avoid the limelight as studiously as he has in the past, but, anyway, I do not believe that "Connie" would sell Collins at that price. And certainly no tail-end club, the kind that needs players most, could afford to pay it.

Mack has a great individuality. He is a crafty, quiet manager who is always under cover and who rules his team with all the authority of a czar, but by persuasion and not the iron hand. He is a very fatherly man, not only with his players, but with his acquaintances, and his men treat him with the respect due a father. He is never one of the fellows on the club. And during a game he is constantly on the job managing, and it is his managing and shrewd judgment which win for the Athletics.

Yet Mack's methods do not seem to prevail when they are absorbed by one of his players, and then the attempt is made to apply them in leading some other team. Take the case of Harry Davis, the old first baseman of the Athletics. When he was Mack's first lieutenant in Philadelphia before he went to Cleveland, everybody regarded him as Mack's reflection and a man who had been a student of the Mack methods for so long that he was almost "Connie" himself. But Davis went to Cleveland as manager and was a rank failure. The explanation of this is that he endeavored to apply the Mack methods to a lot of tough old birds of baseball who had no notion of treating Davis like a father and who resented the constant bossing. In other words, Davis did not have the same atmosphere to work in, because Mack hand-raises most of his players and gets them used to his methods while they are sitting on the bench. Davis attempted to make old-timers like Lajoie and the rest accept the same doctrine instanter. Davis over-managed and the club was all torn up into factions when Stovall took charge of it toward the end of the season after Davis got through.

Stovall made quite a reputation for himself as a manager, because the Naps won a lot of ball games after Davis left. As a matter of fact, Stovall did no managing, but permitted the players to do whatever they thought best as the different situations confronted them, and most of them, being veterans, played the game right. Stovall received credit for doing considerable managing when, as I have said, he did none at all. After he had been in command for a couple of weeks, the Detroit club played a series in Cleveland.

"How do you like managing, George?" I asked Stovall.

"I'm not doing any managing," he replied frankly. "I'm letting all these birds play as they please and getting away with it."

The secret of managing is all in sizing up the men and handling them properly. Now, I am a great admirer of "Hughie" Jennings, but his methods are in great contrast to those of "Connie" Mack. Jennings is a hurrah fellow, with everything out in front. He is never under cover and likes to pat his players on the back and be one of them. He believes in constant encouragement to spur along his men and keep them in a good humor. Neither does he bawl out players much, and never for taking chances. I have been criticized for going to the bat and not bunting when the second guessers in the stands believed that to lay it down was the thing to do. They have roasted me and charged that I was playing for my record, and not the team's. On these occasions Jennings has ordered me not to bunt.

All great managers have one quality. They stick to their men through thick and thin, and are ready to assume the blame for mistakes if a player tries to follow their orders. In this way they get the respect of the players. Members of the New York Giants have told me that McGraw is a great stickler for obedience, but that he never bawls a man if the player tries to follow his orders. Hence, McGraw receives implicit obedience.

"Do what I tell you to, and if things go wrong I'll take the blame," says McGraw. And the players know that he will, and does, and they act accordingly.

The real managers never try to alibi themselves out of their mistakes. The failures are the ones who pursue this course of self-excusing. I know of a leader in the Big League who has never climbed very high with his team. He was never wrong in his judgment. He admits it, himself. But any time one of his pitchers is being hit, this manager blames the catcher, saying he was calling for the wrong kind of ball. It is not the result of the manager's bad judgment in picking the pitcher—of course not.

Now Big Leaguers recognize only two kinds of pitched ball. They speak of the curve and the fast one. A curve is what is called a drop in some other circles, while the fast ball is thrown without any attempt to curve it, but the pitcher puts all his speed on this one. Of course, it does not travel exactly straight, as it is impossible to throw a ball without its curving some, but on the fast ball there is a hop or jump. This manager I have in mind was in the habit of "riding" one catcher in particular who happened not to be going very well one day. A batter got a hit at a critical point in the game, and the manager was sore when the catcher came to the bench, as the hit had resulted in a couple of runs.

"What did you give that fellow?" asked the manager.

"A fast one," replied the catcher.

"You ought to know better than to give him a fast one," the manager snorted. "Always was a fast-ball hitter. Should have been a curve."

"Well, it was a curve," retorted the catcher, with a malicious grin. "But I wanted to cross you up and see what you would say. If I had told you first it was a curve ball, you would have said it should have been a fast one."

The manager roared around a little bit and grumbled a lot, but he had no come back. He made a lot of talk over ball players being fresh and said how they would get along better if they paid more attention to business.

The same manager pulled another funny one which showed up his baseball knowledge, although the play as planned did not work out because of a lucky break. He happened to have one of the smartest catchers ever to horn into the Big League working for him at the time, but he did not realize how valuable this player was and has since let him go. The catcher went to a team which won the pennant and took part in a world's series. He did the bulk of the catching for his club in that big series, too. The pennant-winning manager considered him to be shrewd enough in handling pitchers and attending to his own duties for that.

There was a man on first base and two out, with two strikes on the batter, this day I have in mind, when the catcher was working for the alibi manager. It was the situation and stage at which most any base runner would try to steal. The catcher signed his pitcher for a pitchout so that he would have a better chance to get the man at second with the throw. The twirler was so fixed with this count on the batter that he could afford to waste one, anyway. The runner started, as the catcher thought he would, and the pitchout was the proper thing to do. However, the batter was a pretty shrewd player himself, and he saw the runner get under way out of the tail of his eye. In spite of the fact that he had two strikes on himself and was taking a chance on fanning, he threw his bat at the ball, the pitchout not being very wide, which was no fault of the catcher's. By luck, the bat hit the ball and it bounced off the stick to right field for a clean single. The right fielder, being surprised, fumbled, and the runner, a fast man, scored from first base. The manager let out a terrible roar from the bench. After the next batter had been retired and his team came back to the bench, he began to bullyrag the catcher.

"What did you give that fellow who hit that one to right field when he threw his bat at the ball?" he demanded of the catcher.

"It was a pitchout," replied the receiver. "I figured on that runner going down."

"You should have known better than to call for a pitchout then," stormed the manager. "Why didn't you cross him and stick one over? That's no way to play the game."

"And, if I had," came back the catcher, "you would have been kicking because it wasn't a pitchout if the runner had stolen the base. You're never satisfied unless a play goes through right. Otherwise, a player's judgment is bad."

Managers of this type are never successful. It is not alone because they do not understand the fine points of the game as it is played in the Big League, but also because they do not have the respect of their players. No man can get obedience if he has not respect, and by such tactics a manager only makes the players laugh at him.

The marvel manager of the Big League, to my mind, is George Stallings, the leader of the Boston National League Club. He has great ability for getting baseball out of what looks like a bad club. He took the New York Americans several seasons ago, when they were down at the bottom of the league, and pulled them up to second place before he got into a jam and lost out. He is a team builder. But probably his greatest achievement to date was his showing with the Boston Nationals.

Wilbert Robinson, formerly the coach of the Giant pitchers and now the manager of the Brooklyn club; "Bud" Fisher, the cartoonist, and I were all on a hunting expedition in January, 1913, at Stallings' place in Athens, Ga., which is not far from my home: that is, we hunted in the day-time and talked baseball at night. "Robbie" and I were out hunting one day and, coming back home, we began to discuss Stallings' ability.

"I think he's a wonder," declared Robinson. "He took the worst looking gang of ball players I ever saw last spring and made a team out of them that finished at the top of the second division."

"He did the same thing with the Yankees," I replied. "That New York club certainly looked bad when he took hold, but he lifted them up, and he developed a lot of good ball players for Farrell. He knows ability, and he knows how to handle men. He'll take a lot of sleepy-headed players and have them fighting when no other manager has ever been able to get them to do anything except to eat three meals a day."

"You could not tell whether some of those Boston players were Big Leaguers or tango dancers before Stallings got the team," declared "Robbie." "He certainly woke them up."

"He puts everything that he has into his job," I said. "I have seen him, when he was managing the Yankees, tear all over the bench at a 'bone' play, running the risk of picking up a splinter, but he does not find fault with a plain error. And he can ride players. He keeps them hustling all the time. He is a hard loser himself, and he makes his team hard losers."

Stallings is a real manager, no doubt about it. He is the absolute boss of his men at all times, and while some of his players may not like him, they know that what he says goes. He also has a bad tongue when he goes after a player.

There are almost as many styles in bossing a team as there are managers. Some leaders give their players a good deal of leeway. Frequent disputes have come up recently as to whether the Athletics of to-day or the old Cubs under Chance were the better ball club. Twice I have played against the Cubs in world's series, in 1907 and 1908, and their tactics were the most aggressive of those of any team I have ever seen in action. The players were always fighting and wrangling among themselves, and I thought there would be several fist fights from the names they called each other, yet how they did play ball together, as our club realized from the results of those series. They were all "crabbing." Chance was beefing and calling names, especially with his pitchers.

On the other hand, the Athletics never say much. They simply play the game. "Connie" Mack gives his men a fairly free rein, because he had brought most of them up with two or three years' schooling on the bench and they learn what is right to do under certain conditions.

Although Mack has never liked me since he accused me of purposely trying to spike Baker in Detroit when we were fighting it out with the Athletics for the pennant toward the end of the season of 1910, I have several good friends on the Philadelphia club. Mack got the Philadelphia fans down on me by a statement to the effect that I had tried to cut Baker, and the next time the Tigers played the Athletics in Philadelphia I went to the bench and told "Connie" that I did not believe he had given me a fair deal. These friends of mine on the Athletics, however, have talked over their system with me, but of course without giving away any pointers that would be used against the club.

"Does 'Connie' say much to you fellows?" I asked Ira Thomas one day.

"During a game," replied Thomas, "he lets most of us use our own judgment when we go to bat or are on the bases, unless it is some kid player. He never says much if we are winning, but he talks a good deal some days when things are not going right."

I have heard a player ask Mack what he should do when he was going to the bat and have heard "Connie" reply:

"Use your own judgment." This is his usual answer.

But he never finds fault with a man for what he does if the play goes wrong after "Connie" himself has put it up to him.

"You did all right, old boy," he will advise later, even if he thinks right down in his heart that it should have been worked differently, "but the next time, under the same circumstances, I would try it this way."

Then he goes ahead and gives his reasons for his different point of view. "Connie" is always careful never to break the heart of a young ball player. This is the great mistake made by so many managers. Once a youngster's heart is broken he never comes back. Mack believes in treating them right in their youth. They tell a story of how he handled Wyckoff, a young pitcher, when he went through and won the hardest game he ever pitched on the morning of Decoration Day, 1913. Wyckoff was working against Ford when Ford was at his best, which is exceptionally good.

"We hadn't got anything that looked like a hit off Ford for eight innings," one of the Athletics told me in discussing this game. "He had wonderful speed, and he could put his spitter where he wanted it, and it was breaking a foot wide. It was a tough game to set any pitcher in, let alone a youngster, but once he had started Wyckoff, "Connie" did not want to take a chance on pulling him out for fear the youngster would think his manager had no confidence in him. But between every inning Mack talked to Wyckoff, sitting next to him on the bench with his arm around his shoulders like a father. I could not hear all he said, but I caught scraps of the conversation that went on between various innings.

"'This bird is going pretty strong now, but he's not a full-distance traveler. Just hang on out there, and we'll get some runs for you,' I heard 'Connie' say once.

"It was the ninth inning before Murphy got a hit through the box. The next batter lined to Peckinpaugh, and he should have had Murphy as flat-footed as a cigar Indian off first base for a double play if he had thrown. But he didn't, and lost the double. Hartzell fumbled the next hit, and the old ball game was won for Wyckoff.

"'What did I remark to you?' 'Connie' said to Wyckoff after the game. 'I told you to stick and you would win. That's some pitching, boy.'

"'Connie' was more tickled over the kid winning that game than I ever saw him over anything before," concluded my friend.

The Athletics are a clannish crowd and guard their secrets closely, especially when they think that they have found out something about an opposing club that they can turn to their advantage. Frank Smith, the former spitball pitcher with the Chicago White Sox, used to have a peculiar habit that tipped a batsman off to when he was going to throw his spitter. Of course, whenever a spitball pitcher bluffs at throwing the wet one, he puts his hands up to his mouth just the same, so as to fool the batsman. Then he shoots up a fast one. Now this Smith used to put his hands up to his mouth when he was going to use his fast ball, but he would not look at the ball. But when he really wet it, he would always look at it, so that it was a cinch for the wise hitter to know when a spitter was coming. The Athletics discovered this, along with several other teams in the league, but each club was keeping the fact a secret, believing that it was the only one profiting by it. After this had been known for some time, "Eddie" Collins wrote a story for a magazine after the season of 1910. In it he mentioned this peculiarity of Smith's. I did not see the article, but I heard about it.

"The other fellows on the club gave me the devil for pulling it," "Eddie" told me afterwards. "They said I was not only tipping Smith off to his own weakness, but that I was wising up every club in the league so that they could all hit him and win games from the White Sox."

"Why every club in the league has known about this as long as you fellows have, 'Eddie,'" I told him. "Don't let that worry you."

The winning of two or three championships often demoralizes a team even if the material is as good as ever. After a victorious season, managers say it is hardest to keep players on their toes and hustling. I believe it is due to this reason that no team ever took more than three pennants in succession. The players get too sure of themselves and begin to believe that they know all the baseball there is to know and that no one can tell them anything. In other words, they become blasé. Look at the Athletics of 1912. They were satiated with victory after have won two world's championships in 1910 and 1911, and they became careless. They felt sure that they would win in the end once they got started, and so they never got started. Some of the pitchers and several of the other members of the team were careless about keeping in condition. I remember how sure the

Athletics were up to within a couple of months of the end of the race.

"Oh, the Red Sox will crack and we'll get them yet," one of the pitchers told me toward the middle of August.

But the Red Sox did not crack, and the members of "Connie" Mack's team missed the world's series money in the winter. They had been used to it for two years. They made up their minds to take no chances last season and were hustling from the getaway.

The Cubs were over-confident in 1909 and were beaten out by Pittsburgh, while the Giants of 1906 ran away with themselves after having won the world's championship of 1905. Jennings, who is a great friend of McGraw's, has told me that the Giant leader thought it would be a good idea to give his world's champions a little more leeway in 1906 after having won the high honor the preceding season. During the year that the Giants took the world's championship, McGraw had adhered to his regular plan of campaign. He is one of the strictest bosses in the business, and not a Giant steals a base during the regular season or lays down a bunt or tries the hit and run, or, in fact, does anything else, without direct orders from McGraw, unless he desires to absorb a fine. In 1906, however, McGraw put it up to his men.

"'Mac' says they ran wild on the bases," Jennings told me in discussing it. "They tried all sorts of plays at the wrong stages."

Mack's achievement in winning the world's championship in 1913 with a pitching staff of two veterans and the rest youngsters was a wonderful performance. The man on whom "Connie" had depended to do all the heavy pitching, John Coombs, was out for the season. But both Bender and Plank were in excellent condition, and they were at the top of their form all though the race. Mack campaigned through his schedule depending on his hitters and the judicious switching of his pitchers. The records show that "Connie" changed pitchers one hundred and twenty-three times in the season of 1913. Griffith, who is a great believer in the constant yanking of twirlers, pressed him hard, changing one hundred and twenty-two times.

Griffith is a funny manager and his record shows the inconsistencies of baseball. In Cincinnati his rating was low, but he went to Washington and took hold of a second-division team. He made out of it a pennant contender in one season and finished second. Many a time I have heard Griffith's pitchers complain because he keeps them warming up so much during a game in case he needs one to relieve the man who is in the box.

"We work one day a week in the box and five in the warm-up pens," I heard one of Griffith's pitchers complain once when "Griff" himself was nowhere in the neighborhood to hear him.

Griffith also has a bad habit of nagging opposing pitchers from the coacher's box, especially a young pitcher. He is a fine fellow off the field, but he surely has a nagging manner during a game.

There has been a lot of hard feeling between the Athletics and Washington for some time. It is attributed to two or three causes by the baseball gossips. Some say that Griffith had bets with some of the Philadelphia infielders that his club would beat the Athletics out in 1912. "Griff" finished second and the Athletics third. The story is that "Griff" has never been able to collect his bets and so he "rides" these men about it whenever the Athletics play a series with the Washington club. Especially he "rides" them when Walter Johnson is pitching, because they don't hit much then as a rule, and it is simple to get a man's "goat" when a team is not hitting. There is also a story to the effect that "Eddie" Collins and Gandil got into some sort of a jam because Collins was accused of giving the Washington first baseman the knee as he slid into second base and the knee broke Gandil's nose. The Washington newspapers carried big stories blaming Collins for this, and the Washington fans have been sore at him ever since, although Gandil declared later that the Philadelphia second baseman was not to blame.

Griffith is a smart manager—and a great talker. He declared before the season opened last year that with one good left hander he would loaf to the pennant.

"Give me just one good southpaw, and I'll walk in," lamented "Griff" before the season opened. "But there is not a chance. They have practically stopped building reliable southpaws. I have searched the country and can't find one."

Then "Joe" Boehling, a youngster who pitches from his south side, and who had been farmed out by Griffith, cropped up and made a sensational run of victories. "Griff" failed to win his pennant, however, but he was in there trying and his was a hard club to beat. Now he claims that if he can ever horn into a world's series before Walter Johnson gets all crippled up with hardening of the arteries and other diseases of old age, he will win easily. And I don't doubt but that he will with Johnson fit to work every other day, and perhaps every day if the successive assignments become necessary.

Good baseball managers are scarce. "Connie" Mack's board of strategy has been told about so frequently that it is foolish to repeat a description of its workings here. And "Connie" listens to this board. He favored working a certain pitcher in the fourth game of the 1910 world's series in Chicago after the Athletics had taken three straight, but the majority of the board of strategy advised against it, so he started Bender and the Indian was beaten. The man he had in mind was Coombs, who had already won twice in the series. The board of strategy held that Coombs should have one more day's rest and "Connie" bowed to the judgment of his players. But several members of the board wanted him to put a batter in for Plank on that now famous occasion of the one world's series game which the Giants won in 1913, when the Athletics had three men on the bases and one out in the ninth inning, with a single run needed to win. But "Connie" sent Plank to the bat, and the Athletics lost the game. Still, the pinch hitter might not have done any better and then Mack would have been up against it for a pitcher. The second guessers can always make the best guess.

"Connie" takes care of his young players and will guarantee their conduct to their parents if they want it. They tell a story about "Connie" letting go a fellow who looked like a pretty good pitcher.

"Why did you pass that bird up?" somebody asked Mack.

"Well, his habits were not good, and he was leading some of my young players the wrong way," answered the wily "Connie." "I would rather lose one player than have three or four ruined. I owe it to their folks to keep them straight."

No other manager went over Mack's judgment and signed this pitcher and he is still in the minors. "Connie" is the shrewdest manager in baseball, in my opinion. And, as I have said, good ones are scarce. The job is no bed of roses, either. A fellow bossing a Big League ball club is busier than a one-armed paperhanger with the flying hives.

CHAPTER VI

Facing Tough Breaks in the Big Leagues

Every contest that a Big Leaguer enters is a tough one. But there are some in which the nervous strain is terrific. The Detroit club won the pennant in 1909 in a drive to the wire during the last two weeks of the race, and I have tried to describe in this article the attitude of some of the players under the strain. There never was such a fighting, "crabbing" ball club as that Detroit crowd in those stormy days. How one contest went seventeen innings to a tie, and a player was threatened bodily injury for an error if the Tigers had lost the game and the championship through it.

Many fans believe that the life of a ball player is an easy one, and that the hours are the best which can be had, but these fans are surface thinkers and do not figure on the long jumps, the morning practice, and the nervous strain. I have been asked to write on the "Toughest Situations of My Career." Right here I will probably surprise my readers with the statement that every game, each contest I enter, is tough for me. There is no such thing as an easy ball game.

But I suppose that in the mind of every ball player some few situations stand out as being the crucial ones, and on their outcome

I play games over in my sleep.

has depended largely his future ranking in the game perhaps, along with his team's ultimate standing in the race. These occur most often when a young player is just breaking into the Big League, although I reckon that nearly every ball player enters each game with the notion that he cannot afford to fall down, because there are generally many clamoring for the place. This is especially true of the younger men who have just been assigned to regular jobs, but who are not sure whether they are going to hold them or not, and also of the veterans when they begin to slow up. Aside from the natural anxiety over the outcome, it is this uncertainty about the job which results in the great nervous strain of each game if a man has a fretful temperament.

I don't suppose that Fred Merkle of the Giants will ever forget about the time he failed to touch second base, or if he could the fans would not permit him to on account of their constant howling at him. Neither do I expect that Fred Snodgrass will ever be able to let the incident of the muffed fly in the final game of the world's series of 1912, between the Giants and the Red Sox, which cost a world's championship, slip from his memory. Those were two tough situations. There have been countless others. They have cropped up in the career of every ball player and manager. Skimming over two or three more that come to mind, there was the time that "Connie" Mack was up against the question of whether he should send in a pinch hitter for Plank in the second game of the world's series last fall. Chance faced a bad outlook when he went into the extra game in the season of 1908, and it was put up to him to select a pitcher. On this selection would probably hang the championship and the chance at a world's series purse. As a matter of fact, the game broke so that he could work two pitchers, starting with Pfiester, the old southpaw, and swinging in Mordecai Brown later.

Frequently I have been asked what the toughest situation of my career was. In my baseball days there has not been one, but several. The toughest series of situations occurred toward the end of the season of 1907, when the Detroit team was fighting for the pennant, which it finally won after one of the most trying finishes ever made by a ball club. I broke into the Big Leagues in 1905, so that I was practically a youngster at this time, when the Tigers took their first pennant. Jennings won that championship with the Detroit team in the final two weeks of the season, most of the games being played on the road. If I remember rightly, we had to win twelve out of fourteen battles to take the flag, and we did it.

The reader should be interested in the mental attitude of the ball players under such a strain. We realized that a final victory meant a lot of money in the pocket of each member of the club whether we won or lost the world's series. Aside from this there was the glory that would go with it. During those final two weeks every member of the team was "crabbing." I don't believe there was a pleasant look given or a kind word spoken by anybody. If a man made an error, the rest of the club was ready to do him bodily harm should it cost the victory. In fact, there were several fights between members of the team as the result of nerves drawn tight and to an edge. If a mistake cost a contest, each player thought he had been done some personal injury, intentionally directed at him, which, of course, sounds ridiculous to the normal mind, but we were not normal then.

I recall a game against New York at this period that looked like ours up to the seventh inning, when one of the fielders lost an easy double play, which he would doubtless have accomplished without trouble if the situation had not been so pressing. This oversight put our opponents in a position to tie the game up with a hit that was forthcoming, as is always the case, I have found, under such circumstances. With the game tied, the other club won in the eighth. As soon as the Tigers reached their dressing-room, we all went after that player.

"If we did not have a lot of paralyzed men on this club, we might have a chance at the pennant," squawked one player. "Why didn't you get that double? I've a good mind to knock your block off."

"If you do, you'll get your hands full of splinters or shatter them on the concrete construction," declared another surly player as he stripped off his uniform. "What's the use in us fellows hustling when some bonehead is going to kick the old ball game away from you?"

"If you guys had made as many hits as I did to-day, we would have taken it," replied the player under fire.

"Yes, but you hit them all with two out and nobody on," cracked another one.

"How am I going to hit them with anyone on, if you fellows can't reach the bags?" was the retort.

"You're yellow. That's what you are," cut in the sorest player of all, who was the man that had pitched the game. "You threw me down."

"Yellow" is a fighting word in the Big Leagues. The player who had been put on the rack attacked his accuser, and there was a general muss, which Jennings and the trainer stopped with difficulty.

"Listen, boys," said "Hughey [sic]," who was the balance wheel of the club during those stormy days, "you can't win a pennant if you are going to hurt each other and smash the team all up."

"We'd be better off without that stiff," growled the disappointed pitcher.

"Shake hands with him or you'll be fined," ordered Jennings, who can be a disciplinarian when he thinks the occasion demands it. After much persuasion, and a few cold baths, we cooled off and the quarrel was patched up.

On the other hand, if a pitcher won for us consistently during those trying days we idolized him and could not do too much for him. "Wild Bill" Donovan did some great work in that final rush for the flag. The other players would not let him do anything for himself. If he walked out to the box and forgot his glove, some man, perhaps one of the stars or perhaps a substitute, would rush to him with it. We were all ready to wait on a man who would win for us, and all were prepared to hop on one that could not win. Each wanted to be a valet to a winner. We were what is known in the Big League as a "crabbing" club.

VI. Facing Tough Breaks in the Big Leagues

In this mad rush for the flag the fight was drawn down to a fine edge in that momentous contest in Philadelphia which ran for seventeen innings, and finally decided the championship. That whole contest still stands out in my memory as plainly as it did the night after the game. I recall what a surly crowd we were when we went to the ball park that afternoon. My whole body was weary from the days of fighting those everlasting battles. The nervous strain had been terrific, and many of us had not been sleeping well at night. When I am under a big strain, it is always hard for me to get my nerves straightened out after I go to bed. The old situations keep flashing up, and I play the games over in my sleep, dreaming continually. I wonder if we might not have won if the batter had sacrificed in a certain spot instead of trying the hit and run, and bumping into a double play. A great many of the other players were in the same frame of mind. One man in particular had great trouble in sleeping. I roomed with him, and he would toss about for half of the night and never seem to settle into a sound sleep, but would talk to himself, mumbling away.

I had been out to the theater one evening and came back to the hotel about eleven o'clock. It was during this same Philadelphia series in which the seventeen-inning game that I am going to talk about later, took place. When I got into the room on this night, I found my roommate lying on the bed, fully dressed, with all the electric lights turn on, so that our quarters were lit up like Luna Park for its opening. I thought that he had probably dropped down on the bed for a minute and, out of sheer exhaustion and fatigue, had fallen asleep. I went to the bed and shook him by the shoulder.

"Get up and get undressed," I said. "You've fallen asleep with all your clothes on and you'll feel rotten to-morrow."

"I wish you wouldn't bother me, 'Ty,'" he complained drowsily. "If I undress and go to bed, I get to thinking I won't be able to sleep and begin to worry for fear I will stay awake, and I do, of course. But by throwing myself down on the bed, all dressed, I fooled myself and fell asleep. I am going to stay this way as long as I can. You go to bed in the other room."

When I arose in the morning, he was undressed and in his bed.

"How long did you sleep with your clothes on?" I asked him.

"Until three o'clock," he replied. "Then I had become so used to the exercise that I took a chance and undressed."

That was the most peculiar cure for insomnia I ever heard of, but the beauty of it was it worked, while I have counted sheep jumping over a wall for hours without getting any results.

This story is related to show how a big strain in a pennant race affects the players. Most fans believe that ball players are just big, healthy animals with no nerves and no other tastes off the field except for eating and sleeping. This is not true. Of course, many men in baseball are nerveless, as in every other business. We had them on our club during this final fight for the flag in 1907. But the high-strung player generally finds it difficult to sleep if the race is very tight. That is the reason so many players make a much poorer showing in the world's series than their records throughout the season would indicate they should. The worry over the tough situations they know they are up against keeps them from sleeping soundly. I heard McGraw say just before the last world's series:

"I wish my players would forget baseball, except during the games. But you can't get some of them to keep it out of their minds for a minute. They even dream about it, and most of them don't sleep well. They spend their time reading all the newspaper accounts and criticisms, and these bother them and keep them from composing themselves when they go to bed."

Frank Baker, of the Athletics, is of the directly opposite type. He has no nerves. For this reason he always goes better in a world's series than during the season, because the big games act as a stimulant to him. He tries harder. Nothing worries him. Therefore, he usually bats more than four hundred in the big games, while he does not touch that mark in the regular season, as a rule. The Athletics came to New York from Philadelphia for the first contest of the world's series in the fall of 1913 at about ten o'clock on the night before. They went at once to the hotel where they were stopping, and, as I was doing some newspaper work, I ran up there to see some of my friends on the club and to look the bunch over. Several of the boys were hanging around the lobby.

"Where's Frank Baker?" I asked Ira Thomas.

"Oh, I guess he's upstairs in the hay by this time," answered Ira. "You can't keep that boy up when he knows there is a bed waiting for him. He never broke a date with Morpheus in his life."

Taking my cue, I went to Baker's room to see the great third baseman. He was rooming with "Eddie" Plank and "Wallie" Schang, the young catcher. Baker was ready for bed.

"How do you feel, 'Bake'?" I asked him.

"All right, 'Ty,' but I want to get some sleep if these fellows around here will ever go to bed and give me a chance."

"Think you are going to win?"

"We'll bust them," answered Baker. "We'll bust them wide open. Now, mark what I say."

"Well, I think I'll go along," said I. "Good-night, Frank, and good luck to you."

"Say, 'Schangie,'" I heard Baker yelling at the young catcher as I waited for the elevator outside the door of his room, the transom being open, "get undressed and go to bed so we can put the lights out. I'm tired."

There was not a nerve in Baker's body. He was thinking only of his comfort and not of the tough game next day, as any world's series contest is bound to be. And he went out and played marvelous ball, making another home run.

Next, being a good reporter, or perhaps fair, and, anyway, knowing what a reporter should do, I sauntered down Broadway to the hotel where the baseball headquarters in New York were during the series. In the lobby stood Charley Herzog, the Giant third baseman, nervously playing with a toothpick. His eyes were wide and in them no hint of sleep lurked. I realized at once how he felt. I had seen ball players of this type before. He was all nerves and thinking of the next day. To sleep for him would be a battle. He put up a good front, however.

"How are you, 'Herzy'?" I asked him.

"Pretty good, 'Ty,'" he replied.

"Just left Baker," I volunteered. "He was going to bed. He says he expects to straighten out a few in the series."

"Tell him that I am hitting them hard past third this year," answered Herzog, "and that I am liable to bam a few down there he'll have to give the old how-do-you-do to."

When one ball player talks about giving a hit the "how-do-you-do," he means that it comes so fast he has no relish for getting in front of it and that it is really too warm to handle.

"Going to bed pretty soon, 'Charley'?" I asked Herzog.

"Not just yet," he answered. "I don't feel very sleepy."

Herzog was feeling the strain, and he made a poor showing in the game next day, and, as a result of the bad start, he did not go well during the remainder of the series. He is the sort of player who frets when he gets away bad and is always afraid he is not going to do himself justice. Generally he doesn't, in this frame of mind. Herzog got away to a good start in the 1912 series with the Red Sox and played bang-up ball all the way. This shows the difference in the way that men face tough situations when confronted by them.

VI. Facing Tough Breaks in the Big Leagues

Now, to return to that momentous seventeen-inning game in Philadelphia in 1907 which we left in the beginning of this story while going to the ball park with the Detroit club, and on which hung the championship, as later events proved. As I said, I never felt so weary in my life as at that time. It seemed as if nothing short of a "shot in the arm" would carry me through an ordinary game, and I would have been sure that I could never have gone for seventeen innings if I had known beforehand what was ahead of me. To use the inelegant phrase of the Big League, my coat-tails were dragging before the contest started.

That is a strange thing about baseball. On some days, when I have felt weary, I have played the best ball of my career. Before these contests, I did not feel as if I had energy or life enough to lift an arm. Yet all this weariness appears to slip off me with the excitement of the battle, only to return redoubled after I take off the uniform. Once, a couple of seasons ago, I had an attack of malaria while the Detroit team was playing in New York. My fever ran up to one hundred and four every afternoon, but I did not dare quit, because I was battling for the hitting leadership of the league, and I was afraid the fans would say I was "yellow." It was a terrible effort for me to get up each morning. It took me anywhere from half an hour to an hour and a half to muster the courage to climb out of bed. Yet in that series with the Yankees I never played better ball in my life and gained several points for my batting average. On other days, when I have felt as if I could jump over the grandstand without effort and when I have been exuding "pep" from every pore, I have been very bad. I swing the bat with great energy and hit nothing but the ozone.

It is the same with pitchers in the Big League, more true of some than others. "Eddie" Plank of the Athletics is this type of man, and they tell me that "Hub" Perdue of the Boston Nationals is similar in character. Any time either one of these boys complains of a bad arm or a sore whip before the contest look out for some pitching. It is a standing joke among the Athletics. If Plank goes out to warm up alongside another possible pitcher, his catcher will say:

"How does the soup bone feel to-day, 'Eddie'?"

"So sore I can hardly lift it," he replies.

The word is sent to "Connie" Mack, and "Connie" at once decides to start Plank. The great southpaw has received his worst beatings on days when his arm "never felt better." When he went into the last game of the world's series between the Giants and the Athletics in 1913, with a short rest of two days—it's short for him— he said before the contest that he did not think he would be able to carry his arm without the aid of a sling, let lone pitch. But he produced the game of his career. Mack was satisfied that Plank would win as soon as this bulletin was brought back to him on the bench, so some of the players on the Athletics have told me since.

"It's all right, 'Bunny' will work," exclaimed "Connie" with one of his rare smiles. "Bunny" is the team title for Plank.

Perdue, they say, is a consistent complainer of a sore arm. His wing was so wore before one opening battle against the Giants that they hardly got a hit, as I recall it. Before the contest one of the members of the Giants asked him:

"How is the whip this season, 'Hub'?"

"So sore I wouldn't work if there was anybody else," he replied.

To show the strain of this seventeen-inning battle in Philadelphia, I will relate an incident connected with it. A certain Detroit outfielder dropped a fly in the fourteenth inning. It looked then as if this error would cost us the game and the championship. We all came to the bench and threatened to do this player bodily harm if we lost. Jennings endeavored to smooth over the situation, but none of us was speaking to one another throughout the rest of the game. The finish is probably well remembered. The game resulted in a tie when "Silk" O'Loughlin allowed our claim of interference on a fly ball with which a policeman intentionally came in contact. The players were haggard and in no frame of mind to lose. I don't believe that the erring outfielder would have been able to remain on the club had we missed that championship.

The Giants did not treat Snodgrass in the same way when he made his famous error, which is one of the historical spots of baseball. Only a few blamed him, and Matty, who was the pitcher that did all the magnificent work and was probably the man who lost most, said that any man was liable to drop a fly. "Josh" Devore, they tell me, bawled Snodgrass out in the taxicab on the way back to the hotel from the park.

When a man is working for the batting championship, as I have been for the last several seasons, especially if there is such an opponent as Jackson in the league, he faces a bad situation. As I said in a previous story, my eyes bothered me in 1913, and I did not expect to retain the leadership in the averages. Mrs. Cobb was the only member of the family who was certain of the outcome. She insisted all the way through that I would win out. Hereafter, though, I intend to forget the batting averages and just play the old game. I go down twenty pounds in weight each season between the opening and close after I have trained all the surplus off in the spring.

It is a tough situation when players on the same club "ball" you up on plays. There was a man on the Detroit team who failed time after time to score from second on a hit-and-run play when I followed him with a single. It was because he did not make a good enough start off the bag with the pitch, although the play was planned for the purpose of scoring him. He would pull up on third and give the catcher a chance to throw me out at second. This made me look foolish, and as if I was trying for a record instead of making the play as it should be done.

Whenever some easy play is missed, it usually results in defeat in a close game. This is tradition among ball players, and the man who makes it faces a tough one. I could recall numberless incidents of this sort, I mean that, if the batter hoists an easy foul fly and the catcher misses it, the batter usually follows with a hit if a hit at that time is bound to be damaging. Many a time have I seen this on a ball field.

"Now he'll bust one," a player will remark to a fellow after such an error. They all hate to hear one another say this, too. It is also a superstition of pitchers about somebody yelling in the ninth of a close game: "Come on now. Only three more men."

The chances are that the batters will bust the ball all over the lot after that. The superstition is based on the old one of retribution for boasting. Once a pitcher hears that said he believes that the batters have the edge. Managers go crazy when they hear a youngster blurt it out. It is a common yelp of the minor leagues. Jennings put a recruit infielder into a game late last season which proved to be a hot one with the White Sox. Dubuc, the slow-ball king, was working for us, and he had held Callahan's team scoreless for eight innings, while we had garnered one run. The contest took place in Detroit. As we took the field for the ninth this youngster yelled at Dubuc, "Three more men, old boy."

Right there we all seemed to feel that the ball game was gone. The Sox got three runs.

In the extra-inning game and the last one of the 1912 world's series, the Giants all knew that Speaker would make a hit after both Merkle and Meyers had missed his easy foul. Instead of Snodgrass's muff, I consider that this was the crucial play of the game. When I saw that ball drop safe from where I was sitting in the press box, I said to my side partner, a newspaper man:

"'Tris' will get one now sure and break up the game." He did.

VI. Facing Tough Breaks in the Big Leagues

Ford went eight innings against the Athletics on the morning of last Decoration Day without permitting a hit. In the ninth, Peckinpaugh lost a chance for a double play that would have finished the game. After that Mack's team broke up the ball game.

A ball player's actual hours may be short, but he is always facing tough ones in his working time. They tear the nerves out of a man. In fact, I hope to quit the game when I am thirty and go into the cotton business. My age is twenty-seven now.

CHAPTER VII

The Brainiest Men in Baseball

How brains have saved many a close contest, and how slow think-ing has tossed many away. Big Leaguers are always trying to cross up their opponents and do the unexpected. Many men with little natural ability last in the Big League through their quick thinking, while others, with great natural playing ability, fall down because they are always failing to put through the right plays. Frank dis-cussion of the men, with incidents to illustrate the points from actual games in which I have taken part.

Fans will roast a player for an error. Managers overlook mechan-ical errors, but tear into a Big Leaguer for a "bone" play. Often have I seen a man make a "boot" which cost a club the ball game and never hear the manager mention it to him afterwards, while another player will overlook an opportunity that perhaps does not cost the final decision, but he will find his pay envelope lighter when he draws it, because of a fine, and will have his ears massaged with a few choice bits of conversation from the vocabulary of the boss.

"No player can help making a 'boot' sometimes," says Jennings, "but all are supposed to think."

VII. The Brainiest Men in Baseball

The thinking ball player is the one who succeeds because his kind is scarce. A man with brains is more valuable to a club than one with a corpulent hitting average, but nothing upstairs. The combination of both is the ideal one, and very difficult to find. "Jack" Barry, the shortstop of the Philadelphia American League team, is the weakest hitter in "Connie" Mack's infield, yet many managers and other experts rate him to be the most dangerous. He is the balance wheel of the infield and is responsible for many of the lightning-like plays sprung by his team that choke off rallies by the Athletics' opponents. Personally, however, I consider "Eddie" Collins to be the most dangerous man on the Philadelphia team or any other team in either league.

Run your thumb nail down the list of the great stars of the game, and you will find that they are all thinking men, with reputations for shrewdness combined with their natural ability. Look at Collins, Mathewson, Wagner, Speaker, and the rest who have carved niches for themselves in the baseball world. They are the players who are always doing the unexpected which crosses up opponents and wins battles. And right here I want to introduce the reader to some men who are not so well known to the followers of the game, but are recognized by ball players as being valuable assets to their teams because of their brains. Some of these men cover up weaknesses with their wits, which are almost wholly responsible for their Big League existence. Others, without any wonderful natural ability, keep themselves stars by their headwork.

A ball player's opinion of another player is often very different from that of a fan. Some men that the spectators believe are wonders because they pull sensational stunts are not rated very highly by the Big Leaguers, since the men in the game with them appreciate the chances they miss; while other players, almost ignored by the fans, receive a high rating among their fellows.

"Bobby" Wallace, for several seasons the shortstop of the St. Louis Browns, has much of my admiration and respect for his ability. In the first place, Wallace has been working with bad legs for several seasons, but he has been doing as much damage as any shortstop with whole legs, and a team around him of the caliber of the St. Louis Browns, could be expected to do. He is very brainy, and the one man playing shortstop who absolutely knows how to cover the position with the greatest effect all the time. His brains kept him in the game for a long time after he became badly worn and frayed physically.

Wallace started in baseball a good many years ago as a pitcher, and then, when he had lost his effectiveness in the box, he was shifted over to third base, where he was a star. Next he moved to shortstop, which is the position that he plays with the greatest finish, and where I got my real line on him after entering the league. In running back through my mind for the plays Wallace has made against the Detroit team, I do not recall a single instance where he has been guilty of a wrong move. And "bones" generally stand out in the memory, too, in spite of the great number of games a Big Leaguer takes part in each season.

To my mind, "Billy" Sullivan of the Chicago White Sox was one of the smartest catchers ever to work in the Big Leagues. He was a star backstop long after he had lost his speed and ginger, and when he naturally moved about stiff-legged, because the years of service stooping behind the bat had cramped his muscles. Sullivan was always thinking up ways to cross his opponents, which is the secret of shrewdness in baseball. A man must pull the unexpected to cross up his opponents.

I recall one day when we were playing the White Sox, and I was on second base with Crawford on first. Two were out, and I slipped Sam the sign to try for the double steal. We needed two runs to tie the score at the time, and, with men on second and third, a hit would do it. With men on first and second, as we were, a single meant that we would still be one run behind, and it was against the law of chance that there would be two safe hits in succession with "Ed" Walsh traveling at full speed. I got a good start off the bag and dug for third at full speed, figuring, of course, that the play would be made for me as usual. I hooked the base with one toe as I slid in, and was surprised to see that no effort had been made to stop me. I looked around in time to see "Sam" Crawford being tagged out at second.

On this play, the runner on first generally loafs to second, figuring that the ball will be thrown to third in an effort to stop the farther advanced runner going to that bag. Sullivan realized this, figured that Crawford was a slower runner than I was and that he would loaf down anyway, and took a chance. He knew that his chances of getting Crawford at second, with "Sam" not expecting a play there, were better than his chances of nipping me at third, when I was looking for a hard job to make it. The thing worked out as he had planned it, he got "Sam" and retired the side. The same batter who was up when Crawford was put out for the third man of the inning opened next time with a hit, so I figured that Sullivan's brainwork saved the game for the White Sox right there, as we made one run later, and Chicago finally beat us by only a single tally. Believe me, "Billy" won many a battle for the White Sox with his head.

George McBride, the great Washington shortstop, is another player who has made himself a star through the brainy way in which he plays the game. He is neither a hitter nor a baserunner. On his feet, he is not at all fast, but he is always working his head. He will figure a pitcher and work him to the last ditch, and he never takes a chance on the bases unless he has the percentage with him.

"Charlie" Wagner, of the Boston Red Sox, is still another man considered a star by Big Leaguers who has made himself a top-notcher with his brains and not through natural ability. Ball players rated Wagner to be the most valuable man in the Boston infield in the year that the Red Sox won the championship of the world, yet Yerkes and Gardner had more natural ability than the German, I think. But it was his fast thinking that stopped many a rally by opponents, and he was the man who held the infield together and started most of the plays that retired the opposing side, for which the Red Sox were famous that season. I consider Wagner to be the second best shortstop in the American League, with Jack Barry shading him just a little.

It does not sound very well for a man to talk about the plays he himself has made, but I want to bring up one that I used to try with considerable success, and show how I crossed up Hal Chase one day simply through a lucky break I got. It all hinged on the absence of a water cooler in the visitors' clubhouse in the old American League Park in New York.

Jennings framed up this play, with which I was very successful in a close game against the ordinary first and third basemen. If I reached the bag, Crawford, who batted behind me, would bunt as a sacrifice. Instead of stopping at second and getting one base on the bunt, I would whirl along to third, taking the first baseman off his guard and usually beating the ball to the bag, as the first baseman was bound to be flustered and hurry the throw to third, which would often go wild as a result. I worked this play of going from first to third on a bunt nineteen out of twenty-one times one season.

But Hal Chase, in his prime, was an unusual performer, with lightning-like moves. I put this play over on him once, and then he began to make plans to stop me. We had opened a series in New York several seasons ago, and I reached first base on a single. Crawford put down a bunt, and, knowing that the play was coming, I had gotten a good start with the pitcher's windup and whirled around second. By the time the pitcher had fielded the bunt to first I was halfway between second and third, and the baseman, not looking for a play there, was not covering the bag. I had made two on the sacrifice when it should have been for only one bag. That afternoon, after the game, I was thirsty.

"Where's the water cooler?" I asked our trainer.

"There ain't any in here," he replied. "But go in the Yanks' coop."

At the old American League Park in New York the two club-houses adjoined, with the entrances alongside of each other. I walked into the Yanks' quarters and stopped at the water cooler, which was located near the door. Most of the players were hidden from me by the high row of lockers, and I was also hidden from them. I heard my name mentioned as I was getting the drink, and so eavesdropped. This is considered fair in baseball. Chase was talking.

"Cobb made us look like suckers to-day on that bunt play," he said. "To-morrow we'll get him if it comes up. You stick to that bag, and I'll play the ball to third if I get it, without paying attention to the batter going to first."

"All right," replied the man Chase was talking to; the New York third baseman, "Jimmie" Austin. I recognized his squeaking, penetrating voice.

At once, I made up my mind to cross Chase up. I sneaked out of the clubhouse without anybody seeing me, and was glad that the attendant had neglected to put the water cooler in the visitors' clubhouse. I got hold of Crawford.

"Sam," I said, "they have planned to cross us up on that bunt play to-morrow. Chase is going to play in for the ball and throw it to third to get me. Now, when we pull it, you dig for first, and I'll stop at second."

Along about the third or fourth inning next day, I got on first base with a pass. Chase moved in a little closer than usual and then started to sprint with the pitch. The twirler had delivered the ball low so that Crawford would bunt it, as the low ones are the easiest to lay down. A pitcher keeps them high when he desires to prevent a man from bunting. Crawford laid down one toward first base, which was Chase's dish. He pounced on the ball as I rounded second and took a few strides as if to continue on to third. He took the bait and hurled the ball with one of his bullet throws. Austin made a dab for me, but I was back on second, and Crawford was safe on first.

Hal was sore, because he always hates to see a play that he has planned as a cinch go wrong. He is not unusual in this respect. The next time I got down on the bag, he began to "beef" about it.

"Why didn't you go on to third that last trip, 'Ty'? he asked. "Thought that was your favorite move on the old bunt."

"Because I went into your clubhouse to get a drink of water after the game yesterday and heard you issuing instructions to Austin how to make the play," I answered with a grin.

"I knew you must have been tipped off," growled Chase.

"You tipped yourself off," was my answer.

But Chase perfected that play to such an extent that I seldom tried to make two bases on a bunt against the Yankees afterwards if Hal fielded the ball. He is also a great man to play a bunt to third with men on first and second for a force out. This requires great quickness and an accurate throw. It was this play that cost the Yankees one of the best games Russell Ford ever pitched because "Jimmie" Austin was not there on the throw, according to the gossip I got on the game. After the regular league schedules, the Giants and Yankees played a post season series of games in 1910. Matty and Ford got tangled up in a great pitchers' duel, and the game ran along to the eighth inning a tie, the score being 1 to 1. In this round the play came up, and Chase hurled the ball on a bunt to third base to cut off a runner for a force out. Austin dropped the throw, which had arrived in time to accomplish its purpose, and it cost the Yankees the ball game. The Giants won in that inning after two were out.

Chase is a great ball player. He has what is known in the Big Leagues as the baseball instinct. He always seems to know the right thing to do at the right time, but it does not work out successfully with each try, because frequently he thinks faster than his fielders can, and they will find the ball banged at them when they are not covering, or expecting a play. The result often is that the throw is dropped and the beans are spilled. A favorite play of Chase's while with the Yanks was to take a hit with a man on first base and shoot it to second for a force play and then cover the bag in time to get the batter at first. His throwing has always been a marvel to me, and Hal Chase is one of the men I fear most when on the bases.

"Dodie" Bush, the diminutive shortstop of the Detroit club, says that he thinks outfielders should pay admission into a ball park because they have so little to do. But none of us outfielders agrees with him. While we are not busy all the time, or even most of the time, like infielders, please don't let it be forgotten that the outer gardeners save many a game. Nearly every throw an outfielder is called upon to make is important.

Probably the most dangerous base runner in our league is "Eddie" Collins, because he takes chances and does the unexpected. Collins developed a trick a season or two back that got many outfielders for an extra base. He would drill the ball for two bags easy and take his turn at second, slowing up as if to stop, but still being a few feet over the bag toward third. The outfielder would raise his arm to lob the ball to the second baseman, and Collins would be at full speed in five strides on his way to third. By the time the outfielder could pull his arm back again and change the direction of the heave, Collins would be sliding into the bag. Then the man was hurried, being taken by surprise, and half the time the throw would go wide. Collins also worked this when on the bags, frequently making an extra base in this way if the following batter got a hit. After he had put this over on our club two or three times, Jennings hopped on the outfielders.

"Don't any of you guys throw to the base that Collins is occupying after this," he ordered. "Always make your throws one base ahead. That boy has never stopped even if you think he has."

Many managers display shrewdness through stalling. "Connie" Mack is one of the biggest stallers in our league. They tell me that McGraw is a great fellow to stall his way through in the National. After the world's series of 1910, when the Athletics beat the Cubs, much publicity was given to the fact that "Connie" Mack's team got most of Kling's signs, and this report made trouble among the Cubs, according to reports. One of the defeated Chicago pitchers blamed Kling for displaying his signs too prominently, thereby causing him to lose.

"How do you expect a pitcher to win when his catcher is pasting the signs up on a billboard?" was the remark that started the trouble.

"Eddie" Collins has told me that the Philadelphia club got very few signs in that series. It was also reported that Kling tried to scare Collins the first time he came to bat, the Cub catcher figuring Collins to be a comparative youngster.

"Did Kling make any cracks to you?" I asked Collins afterwards.

"No," replied "Eddie." "We never worked against a catcher that treated us better. He never said a word to me."

But crafty "Connie" Mack did not deny the stories that his players were bears when it came to stealing signals. In fact, he did everything that he could to increase the impression by such means as instructing his runners when they got to second base to stand on the bag for a minute before taking their leads, while the opposing catcher was giving his signs and peer as if trying to see them. He also told the coachers at first and third to look wise as if they were accumulating a lot of information. The net result of these tactics is that the Athletics ever since have had their opponents on their toes and worried. It also forces the pitcher to take his mind off his work because he is constantly fretted for fear the batter is wise to what he is going to throw.

The idea that the Athletics steal so many signs is now being rapidly dispelled in our league, however. Jennings has instructed our pitchers, if they think coachers or base runners are stealing the signals, to work fast so that there will be no opportunity for them to be passed to the hitter before the ball is pitched. Besides, most batters are becoming afraid of taking signs, since there is a good chance the information may be wrong and they will be "beaned," the great fear of all base players. Often a man is unable to come back after being hit a hard blow in the head by a pitched ball. Many have been hurt in this way during the past few seasons. It requires supreme courage to come back after this. Chance was "beaned" several times and always came back, but this constant "beaning" got him in such a condition that he became the victim of headaches, which finally crowded him out of the ranks of the regulars. Players who were with Chance on the old Cubs when he was suffering from these headaches tell me he went through hell with them. Finally, they became so severe that an operation was necessary.

McGraw is a great man to kid and to attempt to gain various advantages by letting reports of his methods leak out. For instance, word came to the Athletics before the world's series in which these two teams met in 1911 that McGraw had been tipped off that Frank Baker could be sent high in the air by a verbal attack from the coaching lines. The Athletics were brought to believe that they would be torn in two by McGraw's tongue.

"Was it true?" I asked one of them, a friend of mine, after the series. "Did McGraw have much to say to you fellows?"

"No," was the reply. "He minded his own business and laid off of us. He is one of the squarest managers we ever played against, and we could not have expected fairer treatment in spite of the stories we heard before the series."

Perhaps McGraw had nothing to do with this report, and perhaps he did, thinking that it might give him a little edge if the Athletics believed he was going to pile on them from the coaching lines with his conversation. Anyway, he did not have much to talk about in either series the way the games broke. However, all American Leaguers speak well of McGraw and his methods. His club has been defeated in the last three world's series, and he has always been the first to rush over and congratulate the victor. Do not think this has been an easy task, either, because McGraw is the type of man that likes to win and hates to lose.

After the concluding game of the series last fall, McGraw ran over to the Athletics' bench. First, he stretched out his hand to "Connie" Mack.

"I want to congratulate you, 'Connie,'" he said. "You had the better club again."

Next he reached for Collins' hand.

"Put it there, old boy," he said; "I think you are the greatest player in the world."

They tell a story of a trick that McGraw pulled in the series the Yankees and Giants played in 1910, to which I referred earlier in this article. It was an old hoax of the game, but it worked, which is really what makes any trick worth while. After Austin had dropped Chase's throw and filled the bases in the eighth inning of that first game, which was a pitchers' battle between Ford and Mathewson, Ford fanned Snodgrass, and Murray flied to Hemphill, as I recall the story, which has been told to me often enough. Two were out, and "Al" Bridwell, the former New York shortstop, generally reckoned to be a weak hitter, came up to the bat. It was evident that the strain was telling on Ford, and he threw Bridwell two bad balls. It was here that McGraw, coaching on third base, stopped the game and walked to the plate. He called Bridwell aside from the batter's box and whispered something in his ear. Of course, all the players on the American League club began to wonder what McGraw had said, and it made them a little nervous. Ford let the next one go pretty wild, and Bridwell stopped it with his shin. There was a protest to the umpire from the players that he had gotten hit on purpose.

"McGraw told him to do that," declared the fans. "He's a shrewd guy all right."

As a matter of fact, McGraw had not said anything to him about it. Wilbert Robinson, who was the coach of the Giant pitchers for several seasons, told me the real story of this incident only a few weeks ago when he was hunting with a party at George Stallings' place in Georgia. We got to talking about that game one night, and Stallings, who had been deposed as manager of the Yankees just before this series, declared that he believed McGraw had directed Bridwell to get hit.

"Not at all," answered Robinson, taking the part of his old boss and friend. "Do you know what 'Mac' said to him? He just whispered to Bridwell, 'Do you expect a big crop on the farm next spring?'

"The whole play was a stall to put the Yankees up in the air, and it worked out fine. McGraw thought the game would be won or lost right there, and he took a chance on worrying Ford."

There is almost as much bluffing to baseball as poker, and the best managers are often the best bluffers. "Larry" Doyle, the second baseman of the Giants, is a good friend of mine. I asked him one day during the world's series last fall whether McGraw was a smart manager.

"Is he smart?" asked "Larry" in reply. "Say, he's the guy that wrote both the book and lyrics of managing, as they say in the show business. He knows what you ought to do before the play comes up, and he fines you if you don't do it. I know it cost me ten dollars in a game last season because I took only one base on a hit that he estimated to be good for two.

"'What are you loafing for, "Larry"?' he says to me when I came to the bench later. 'Did you think you were suffering from the sleeping sickness down there on first base? That will cost you ten.' And it did."

On most pennant winning clubs, the players are a shrewd bunch of performers and ready to take advantage of every opportunity. These smart boys, when they get into a tight fight for first place, think of the game all the time, too—off the field as well as on. That is what makes the men on a ball club up there fighting for first place so crabbed. They are always playing the game in their minds. Many followers of baseball do not think that the Giants are a brainy club because McGraw makes all the moves and plans for them all that a manager can for a team and leaves very little to the men. I differ in this opinion. Mathewson is one of the smartest men I ever saw on the diamond. Doyle, Fletcher, and Herzog (now manager of the Reds) are also fast thinkers. Fletcher is one of those men in the National League that players reckon to be far more valuable to a club than the fans consider him to be. Big Leaguers realize the important part he plays around second base, and also appreciate the fact that he goes after everything which comes anywhere near him, and grabs many a drive that would get away from any other shortstop.

VII. The Brainiest Men in Baseball

You never find brains in a ball player who is without nerve or courage. As I have said before, pitchers will test out a player's nerve as soon as a new man breaks into the league, and catchers will aid them in this. If a batter is inclined to crowd the plate, a twirler will shoot one straight for his "bean." The catcher will collaborate on the play with some such remark as, "He 'beaned' one guy last week, and he is in the hospital yet."

If you step back and fail to stand up to the plate on the next pitch after a close shave, all the twirlers in the league are soon on you. One tells another. Several of the pitchers tried this trick on me when I was first breaking into fast company. I made up my mind that they could never say I lacked nerve, so I used to crowd the plate closer after a pitcher had offered me a "bean" ball. That is the only way to do. I also used to come back with a lot of conversation along these lines:

"You're wild enough to work with a bush league outfit. Don't think you worry me by shooting at my 'bean.' I enjoy it. Come on, I want a base on balls."

If a pitcher tries to scare me away from the plate, I fight him so as to put him on the defensive, instead of letting him put me in the hole. If it become known that a hitter is "bat shy," as is indicated when he "sticks his foot in the water pail" after the pitcher aims at his head, all twirlers keep "on him." Then, if he comes up in a pinch when a hit is needed, the first thing the pitcher does is to aim one at his "bean" to scare him away. When a young player comes into the league, all the pitchers search his batting style for a weakness. As soon as one is discovered, the tip goes over the entire league, and all the twirlers aim at it. Everything is done to test and break the young player's nerve before he is admitted to fast company on an equal basis with the seasoned Big Leaguers.

I could name countless men in baseball with great natural ability and no brains. These players will always be mediocre performers because what is above the collar band in a player is worth more in the Big League than what is below it, provided a player is not paralyzed. But I am not going to name any of these men who lack brains because it might cause some hard feelings. They are, however, absolutely dependent on the heads of their managers, and when they have to make a decision which does not give them time to refer to the leader for advice, they generally pull a "bone."

"If that guy's brains were made of nitroglycerin and they exploded the bust wouldn't muss his hair," I heard Jennings remark of a player one day. "Give me a man who can think and with arms and legs, and I'll make a ball player of him."

Yes, it takes brains to make a star in the Big Leagues, as in any other business.

Chapter VIII

Big League Base Running

The aggressive man and the one who does not fear injury is the one who makes a base runner. Infielders attempt all sorts of tricks to prevent a man from reaching a bag. Some of the things that have happened to me, and how I treat a baseman who attempts to block me off. The best base runners in the game, and why.

Many fans believe that the fact that I swing three bats before going to the plate to hit is a mark of conceit. It is not. My original purpose in wielding three bats, of course, was to make the single one feel light after I really got up there to hit, but I have found that this sort of exercise strengthens my back and arm muscles, as well. These have developed wonderfully since I took up the scheme.

One day, just before the Detroit club went into its spring quarters for the preliminary training a couple of years ago, I got to figuring how I could increase my speed and get my legs in good shape to stand up throughout the coming campaign. It seemed as if I might accomplish something by applying the principle of the three bats to my legs, so I took an old pair of baseball shoes and had a shoemaker push some lead slugs into the soles. These I wore throughout the period spent in the spring camp, and also all the way north. They strengthened my legs, and the weakening of the underpinning is the

He would begin to tell a story and talk the player's foot right off the bag and then tag him.

fear of most ball players. The legs of a Big Leaguer generally go first.

With the team was a young newspaper man who was making his first trip to a southern training camp with a Big League club. He was very conscientious about getting his news details, and thought he had made a great discovery in regard to me. He noticed that I was not beating out the same kind of hits that men on the club, rated to be slower than I, were outfooting to first base. We also had some competition in going around the bases one day, and a couple of "bushers" in camp beat my time. We got into Indianapolis early one morning and were to play the American Association team that afternoon. I bought all the Detroit papers, and was surprised to see this heading in the one represented by the young man in question:

"'Ty' Cobb Going Back."

The article went on to tell, in about a column and a half, how I was losing all my speed and, therefore, my value as a base runner. I showed the paper to "Hughie" Jennings, and he only smiled.

"I guess I'll show this bird this afternoon," I told Jennings. "I'll ask the trainer to get out my regular shoes."

"All right, Tyrus," replied Jennings.

The light sprinting shoes I wear when the club is in a championship campaign felt like feathers on my feet after the weighted ones, and it seemed as if I were full of speed that day. Three stolen bases were my record for the afternoon, and the Indianapolis club had a good throwing catcher that year, too.

After the game I dug up the young correspondent.

"What do you think of my speed now?" I asked him.

"How did you do it?" said he, surprised. "I thought you were slowing up."

"I was as long as I wore lead in my shoes," was my reply. "Now, you've got a good story to send to your paper about how I work up my speed for the season."

But this story has never appeared. I consider the idea of wearing weighted shoes while training a good one, and believe it helps me in my base running. I have used the scheme ever since, and intend to repeat the practice every spring. So if you read in the newspapers that I am slowing up any time the Detroit club is in the South, you will know what the explanation of it is.

Base running is one of the most important and yet one of the most neglected parts of a Big League ball player's business. The lack of proper base running ability on a club has kept many a likely team from winning a pennant. The National Leaguers tell me they believe that if the Pittsburgh club had displayed more base running in the past few seasons, it would have been up there fighting for a championship.

"But it takes a cannonade to get a Pirate around the bases," one National Leaguer remarked to me of "Fred" Clarke's team.

In running the bases there are all sorts of tricks to be applied. The basemen are always on the job trying to spring new ones, and a ball player has to think fast to outguess some of the men guarding the sacks. One of the fastest at this is Hal Chase.

When Hal was with the Yankees, he could think of more ways to nip a base-runner than any other man I have ever seen in baseball. He had one trick he used to pull all the time which resulted in the sudden death of many a base runner. If a man was in the paths and the batter hit to the infield, Chase would take the ball as thrown to him at first base by the infielder for the out and then whirl with the speed of lightning and throw it to the bag where the base runner had probably overrun. He tried this on me, and it worked several times. It got me guessing.

Then, one day, I was on second when there was a hit to the third baseman. He shot the ball to Chase and I steamed for third base, which I made handily enough, and which I overran by a good margin on purpose. Chase was watching for this, so I "souped" him along until he shot the ball to the third baseman. I waited until I saw him bring forward the ball to let it go, and then I let out for home. He saw what I was up to just as he let go of the ball, and he hurried his heave. The throw went bad, the third baseman fumbled it, and I scored. That is half of base running—catching the other side off its balance and pulling the unexpected, as it is half of almost any other branch of baseball.

The base runner who is up in the records at the end of the season must know all the tricks of each baseman on the various teams, and every one has many. He must also be familiar with their style of covering the bag and tagging a runner so that he will know the best way to go about it to avoid being put out. It is the outsider who lays the stress upon speed in a base runner. Sprinting ability, of course, is a valuable thing in going around the paths, but the start and finish are far more important. Some of the best sprinters in the world would be poor base runners if they did not know how to get their starts, and were not familiar with the pitching motions of the various twirlers in the league. For instance, if a player can discover some slight move that tips him off when a pitcher is going to deliver the ball, it may mean five stolen bases to him in a season.

In stealing a base I generally watch the baseman's eyes, to make up my mind how to come into the bag. It is useless to try to look at the ball, because, when going down to second, it is then necessary to turn around and watch over the shoulder. This throws a man out of his stride and causes him to slow up. By watching the eyes of the player who is to receive the ball, it is easy to tell on which side of the bag to come in to present the smallest possible area for touching purposes. From a baseman's eyes, I always make up my mind on which side to slide, and I never decide this until I do get a look at them. After I have once made my decision, I never change it, because this has injured more players in baseball than any other one cause, I believe.

If a runner starts to slide in to a base on one side, and then, as he prepares to hit the dirt, suddenly changes his mind, he is liable to come up with a sprained ankle at least, and probably a broken leg. It is almost suicidal to start a slide and then suddenly decide to stay up because there is no play being attempted at the base where you are arriving. It has always been my rule that when I once make up my mind to hit the dirt, I never change it, and I go down traveling at full speed. This is the safest way. The worst you can get as a result of this system are some sliding "gooseberries" and, maybe, a spike wound. But by changing your mind suddenly, you are liable to come up with a broken leg, which never comes around right again and slows you up as a player.

The great secret, to my mind, of being a good base runner is to hit the dirt with the feeling that you like the sensation. In the early months of a championship race, I am always covered with sliding blisters, as the pads are strapped fast to my legs under the uniform and slip when I do. But a player soon becomes toughened to these and has nothing toward the end of the season but some scars and callous spots. It is hardest to get going in the early weeks of the race when the sliding sores are bad, but even then a player must hit the dirt as if he enjoyed it.

Look at the men in baseball who have been hurt for suddenly shifting their opinions. "Mike" Donlin, at an important moment of the race for the National League pennant in 1908, sprained his ankle by trying to stay up after he had started his slide. It put him out of the batting order for some time, and was probably largely responsible for the loss of the championship by the Giants, as the race that year was decided by only one game. "Johnny" Evers was out of the game when he changed his mind about sliding two or three years ago. Harry Wolter of the Yankees broke his leg in the same way. It is a foolish thing to do.

Base running is a dangerous branch of the pastime, and it takes nerve for a man to be up among the leaders. It is not only dangerous for the runner, but frequently for the basemen as well. The collisions at first base, when a player is clumsy about covering, are particularly dangerous, because a runner is not slowing up at all as he crosses the bag. They tell me that after McGraw had the pennant practically won in 1911, he put Arthur Devlin in at first base for a few games in order to rest up Merkle. Now, Devlin was about as slick as anyone at taking care of third, but first was a new beat for him. He was always getting tangled up with the runner and narrowly missing having an arm or a leg or perhaps his neck broken. At last, McGraw called him off.

"Guess you're not meant for that job just yet, Arthur," he told Devlin. "There are three or four guys looking to kill you now because they claim you have been blocking them."

One of the gamest exhibitions at first base I ever saw was the work of George Wiltse for the Giants during the 1913 world's series with the Athletics. After Merkle was hurt, Wiltse went in there with only the little experience he had gained from covering the bag in odd moments of preliminary practice, and made a great showing. He displayed more gameness than any other member of the New York club besides Mathewson and McLean. When the Giants took the ten-inning game from Plank, Wiltse, next to Mathewson, deserved the most credit for the victory. He was steady and game under the fire and battled on in the face of what looked like almost certain defeat. By his fine fielding and throwing, he retired two men at the plate, when, if either one of them had scored, the Athletics would have won the contest. A good first baseman is very important to a ball club.

The Detroit club started out in 1910 and won twenty-six and lost two out of its twenty-eight games. We were away out in front, and it looked like a cinch that we would grab the championship until Coombs hit Gainor, the Tigers' new first baseman, in the arm with a pitched ball and broke it. We had taken the first two games of the series with the Athletics by big scores, but the team began to go bad just as soon as we lost Gainor. It cracked our infield. Even "Connie" Mack said of Gainor:

"He looked like one of the best first basemen I ever saw come into the league."

It is strange how things work out. Toward the end of the 1911 season, after the Athletics were almost sure of the pennant, Mullin, the old Detroit pitcher, broke McInnis's arm and kept him out of the Athletics' lineup for the world's series except for a part of one game. This injury did not damage Mack's team as much as the disabling of Gainor did Detroit, because "Connie" had the veteran Harry Davis to put into the lineup, and Davis never played better ball than he showed in that series. All this has little to do with base running, but it came to my mind under the dangers of the game.

My readers are going to be surprised to hear me say that it is easier to steal third base than second, but that it is not stolen so often for the reason the gain is not so great. When a runner is on second base, he can take a longer lead, because the pitcher has to turn clear around to watch the bag, and, if he is to get his man, he must whirl and throw without looking, taking a signal from the catcher as a rule and depending upon either the shortstop or second baseman to cover. Neither has he any mark to fire at, because the base is being covered by a man on the run. He can just shoot the ball to the bag and must depend upon it that someone is going to be there. Frequently, the throw is bad, or the base is not covered through a mixup, and the ball goes to the outfield. A runner on second can also get a better start for third than one on first. But a man can score from second, if he is at all fast, on a clean hit, and therefore the advantage in stealing third, compared to the chance taken, is not so great.

Many tricks are practiced, both by base runners and the basemen. "Bill" Couglin used to be one of the best conversationalists in the Big Leagues when he was in his prime as a player and talker. He would begin to tell a story and talk the runner's foot right off the bag and then tag him. I saw him get a man one day in this way, and I don't care to mention the victim's name, for he is still in the league. The shortstop had the ball hidden, and Couglin said:

"We had some poker game on the way here last night. There was one pot, that I took, which looked like my salary check, and a pair of aces, combined with a little nerve, did it. Yes, sir. I had all the rest of the bunch backed up."

The base runner and the coacher were both listening. The shortstop shot the ball, and the runner was out a yard. He had become careless and left his foot off the bag, always a bad mistake.

"Come around again and listen to some more of my stories," laughed "Bill," as the crest-fallen runner headed for the bench, and a bawling out from his manager.

There is an old trick, for which I do not desire to claim any credit, that I have often worked successfully from my position in the field, particularly on bushers who are just coming in. Suppose the runner is on first base and the batter puts up a fly to the field. The runner and coacher naturally take a flash at the ball. I act as if the fly were going over my head and stall my way along until the runner breaks for second in spite of the shouting of the coacher. The wise manager keeps shrewd advisers on the coaching lines, but the impetuous youngster frequently fails to heed what they say when he becomes excited. As soon as I see the runner make a break, I get the fly and shoot the ball to the bag for a double play. It may sound like a simple trick, but it works often, and the result is the real test of anything. It is like a story I heard recently about a young fellow who said he asked each girl, as soon as he met her, whether he might kiss her.

"Don't you get in awful bad sometimes?" inquired his friend.

"Some of them do get a little sore," replied this Romeo, "but you would be startled at my average."

You would be surprised at my average in springing this old one on base runners.

In base running much depends on the coachers, as they can see the ball all the time and are able to advise the runner with a word or a motion when he glances at them. It is frequently necessary to depend on a sign from the coacher, as the noise from the crowd is so great that the runner cannot hear what he says. Many base runners get blamed for the mistakes of coachers, and many coachers get panned for the "bones" of a base runner when the latter refuses to pay attention, which is often. On almost every ball club there are some men known as "hog wild" runners, and it is almost impossible to stop them once they get going after the batter has hit. To men of this type, third base is a point at which they hate to pause, and many coachers in the National League will tackle a runner of this kind and throw him back on the bag. I have seen McGraw do this in a world's series with "Red" Murray, but they are stricter about this sort of football coaching in the American League.

To show how important managers consider the directing of the base runners, I am going to relate an incident which occurred in that thrilling world's series of 1912 between the Giants and the Red Sox. All through the summer "Heinie" Wagner, the Boston shortstop, and "Bill" Carrigan composed the board of strategy on the Red Sox club. They always roomed together, and they used to spend their evenings mapping out the campaigns. Stahl would call upon them for advice in almost every game.

When "Buck" O'Brien was picked to pitch the Monday contest in New York after the Red Sox had won three and lost one, "Bill" Carrigan warmed him up with his shin guards on, ready to go in, as he expected to work, because he has been O'Brien's catcher throughout the season. Just before the batteries were announced, Stahl came to Carrigan on the bench and said:

"I guess we'll let Cady catch to-day, 'Bill.'"

"What for?" asked Carrigan.

"We can use you better on the coaching lines."

That is how important Stahl considered his coachers to be. He held the shrewdest player on the team out of the contest when the pitcher he was accustomed to work with was in the box in order that this man might direct the base runners. There is more to this story, and how it worked in disorganizing the Boston club, but it is not up to me to tell the gossip of the league that might reflect on any men and the resultant lack of harmony among the Red Sox.

When a man starts out to steal a base, he must always be aggressive without attempting to hurt or cut anybody. If basemen find a man afraid to slide in hard, they are going to block him off sure. When I go out to steal a bag, I make sure to get my start, the most important part of making the distance successfully, and then I never turn around to see where the ball is coming. I just watch the man covering the base and pull my body away from where he is going to receive the ball. I can always get a line on this from his actions.

There is an old trick that works frequently when runners are on first and third and the word goes out for a double steal. The usual way in which a team will endeavor to break up this double steal is for the shortstop to come in about ten yards in front of the bag to take a short throw from the catcher in case the runner on third starts for home. If he does, the shortstop grabs the throw and returns the ball to the plate. If not he lets the ball go on to the second baseman to make the play for the man who is coming down.

Now if the runner on third is only stalling and does not intend to try to make it home, I always yell at the shortstop:

"Take it! Take it!"

Of course, he is watching the ball and cannot see whether the runner on third has started or not when the play is once under way. Very often, not recognizing my voice, the man, who is not a veteran, will cut in and grab the ball, and the runner gets into the bag standing up. Or if the runner on third starts for home, then I yell:

"Let it go! Let it go!"

The shortstop will often duck and let the ball go to the base. I turn around and dig back for first to give the man going home a chance to score, and the whole defense is upset.

Smart ball players are always figuring out ways to get the base runner, especially if he is a busher and not familiar with all the rough work of the majors. There is an old one pulled by many second basemen and shortstops on recruits. The green one gets down to second base, and the catcher makes a bluff to throw the ball, after receiving it from the pitcher, to catch him napping. The runner scampers back to the bag, which has been covered by the shortstop. As the latter walks toward his position again, he cuts into a conversation with the busher to hold his attention.

"If the catcher'd thrown that time, he would have got you," says the shortstop.

The youngster, thinking this a reflection on his baseball intelligence, turns his head to argue and protest.

"I would have been sitting on the bag when the ball got there," he replies.

The turning of the head is fatal, for the second baseman sneaks to the bag, the catcher shoots the ball, and the runner is out by yards and walks to the bench listening to the laughter of the shortstop who has pulled the trick, and having some idea of what his manager will say to him. He goes to the water cooler first for his drink, as any ball player does after he fans or pulls a "bone," and then huddles down on the end of the bench. But, from the average Big League manager he always gets the call for the "bone," no matter how hard he tries to dodge it.

There is one spectacular play in base running that the fans like to see, and that most managers will "bawl" a player for attempting whether or not he is successful. This is stealing home. When a man starts to steal home, the "percentage" is all against him. I have heard managers call down a man for attempting the play, even after it has been successfully accomplished.

In concluding, I want my readers to appreciate the fact that there is plenty of science in base running. Most teams have a set of signs for this branch of the game that are necessary for its success.

A player must be willing to take chances on the bases. Good base runners are valuable assets to any club, because nothing will keep an opponent guessing so much as a collection of base stealers. Once a team begins to run wild on the paths and steal bases loosely, it usually means defeat for its opponents.

Base stealing and taking chances is the great thing in the Giants' game, and the National Leaguers tell me that they believe the New York club's success in the past few seasons has been due to base running. I have been told that during the last western trip in 1911, McGraw had to send back to New York for some new trousers to dress his players properly for appearance on the ball field. So busy did he keep the boys running the bases that they slid the seats all out of the ones they brought with them. I don't know whether this is true, or whether it was just a story launched from the McGraw camp to throw a scare into "Connie" Mack. Anyway, the crafty leader of the Athletics made preparations and had his catchers drilled to stop any such attack. They did, too.

Players who cannot run the bases are not very valuable to a club. Even if they get on, it takes a lot of safe ones to bring them around home. Base running is as important a department of the game, in my estimation, as any other single branch of baseball.

As I said before, the good base runners are the ones that are not afraid to hit the dirt, and the science of sliding is a large part of successful base running; and most managers, realizing this, rehearse their players diligently in sliding during the spring practice. Nearly all the star base runners, such as Bescher, Collins, Milan, Speaker, and the rest, use the hook slide now. There are only a few left who go into the bag head first.

Fred Merkle, of the Giants, and Hal Chase, frequently take a dive at the base, but whenever they attempt this they are always running a risk of hitting the baseman with their heads and injuring themselves. If a baseman knows that a runner slides head first he is not so apt to give him his share of the lines as he would be if he expected to be met by a pair of spikes. The runner presents a smaller area to touch when he uses the hook slide and throws his body away from the bag. This style requires an expert in tagging to get a man who has perfected the fall-away slide.

Watch the stars of the game next season, and see how they go out to steal a bag. Notice how they get the start and pay no attention to anything until they hit the dirt. To me, it is the most thrilling and absorbing play of the game, and it satisfies me almost as much to steal a base as to drive a ball on a line for a clean hit.

CHAPTER IX

Making a Big League Hitter

It was long believed that a batter had to be born, but there are good stickers in baseball who are what we call manufactured products. "Connie" Mack is a great manager to develop a man into a hitter, and how he has produced some of his. Why one man, as "Joe" Jackson, hits better at home than on the road, and vice versa. Batting also requires quick thinking.

The impression existed in baseball for a long time that a batter had to be born and that this branch of the game could not be learned. I maintain that certain natural qualities must be born in a man to make him a good hitter and that with these he can develop himself into a formidable sticker. I was not always a hard hitter, yet I have had pretty good luck at this end of the game for the past few seasons because I made a study of batting, deeming this to be the most valuable part of a player's work.

Nobody would expect a one-legged man to be a good infielder and to develop into an "Eddie" Collins or a "Hans" Wagner, because the missing leg would naturally be a big handicap. Since a bad eye is not so apparent, many managers and fans find fault with players

Frank must have his sea-food diet.

with weak lamps because they cannot hit. You would be surprised at the number of men playing ball in the Big League who could not get a very high mark if they were to undergo an eye test, and who should be wearing glasses. Of course, none of them will wear them, because that would be a practical admission of weakness.

Many ball players strain their eyes by abusing them. They read in bad light while on the road or otherwise put them to a strain. With a few exceptions, it is almost impossible to get Big leaguers to accept a word of warning, because they believe their eyes are strong enough to stand any test or strain.

"Oh, you can't hurt my glims," protests the abuser.

IX. Making a Big League Hitter

Now, I know that my own eyes are none too strong, and that they gave me a lot of trouble last season, and so I am the greatest little caretaker of the lamps you ever met. I insist on the light being good before I read, and I do very little of it on trains even when the shaking motion is not perceptible, a motion which oculists have told me is a great strain on the eye.

For a long time "Fred" Merkle of the Giants was a voracious reader, and in the winters he used to sit up until late in the night studying the fine print of the law books. This was his hobby. I have heard McGraw make the statement that by using his eyes so constantly Merkle had hurt his hitting.

"Merkel has strained his eyes from reading so much," declared McGraw to a bunch of us in the lobby of the Copley Plaza Hotel in Boston one night during the world's series of 1912. "I can tell by the way in which he misses the ball when he is at bat. It is easy to pick out the players with the bad eyes, and I could tell you about a lot of them in the league who are getting away with it, but they would be hitting much harder if they would take care of their lamps. I believe that all Merkel's eyes need to restore them to their former healthy condition is a good rest."

The Giants' first baseman took McGraw's advice in the winter after the 1912 season, so I am told, and he had a much better year in 1913. From what I can gather about the Giants-White Sox world's trip, Fred did a great lot of hitting on it and amazed several American Leaguers who were on the tour and had seen Merkle's hitting only when he has appeared in a world's series, or who were acquainted with it simply by the accounts they had read in the newspapers.

Sightseeing is not hard on the eyes, and Merkle applied his lamps to this sort of work all winter during the world girdling trip. The evident result has been that his hitting has improved. Many ball players are great moving picture fans, but it is my belief that this sort of amusement hurts the eyes because of the flicker of the films. I know that I don't hit as well the day after I have gone to a "movie" show. As I have said in one of my previous articles, many players use the moving pictures for an alibi.

Therefore, the first natural quality that a man needs to become a hitter is a good eye. After this comes a good, stout heart, for in hitting this is more necessary than in fielding. If the pitchers in a league find that a batter is afraid of the ball and backs off from it, they will keep popping them at his head right along until they scare him out of the box. And don't forget that every recruit who comes to the league undergoes this test. After a good heart and good eye, comes the mind. A player must be a student of hitting, and he must have exceptional judgment in "picking them out" to become a star. No player ever became a great batter by going after bad balls. Pitchers soon find this out and give him nothing else. Concentration on the work in hand is the great thing in batting.

Once I compiled a list of "don'ts" for young batters. Here they are:

Don't try to copy the style of some great slugger. His form may not suit you—probably won't.

Don't pull away from the plate when a pitcher serves a curve ball.

Don't try to kill the ball.

Don't try to place your hits until you have perfected your form.

Don't take your eye off the ball from the time the pitcher takes his place in the box. Sometimes it is hidden momentarily from your view by an eccentric motion. This, of course, cannot be avoided.

Don't let the instructions of the coacher guide you at all times.

Don't be on the defensive when running bases.

Don't slide head first.

When I was in the minors, I was not rated as a star hitter, but

IX. Making a Big League Hitter

I began to figure my faults and to remedy them as I realized what they were. I decided that the great thing to do was to keep the pitcher on the defensive all the time, if possible, and that the way to do this was to outguess him. After a twirler has been outguessed by a batter a couple of times, he's licked by you for the afternoon. If he outguesses you, you're licked. There are many instances of a batter coming into the league a bad hitter and developing himself into a three hundred man by his own shrewdness. On the other hand, often a player will go like a house afire for a month or perhaps six weeks until the pitchers discover what his weakness is and pitch at it. Then he starts back in the general direction of the minors. Frequently a change in form will make a star slugger over night out of a weakling.

The greatest instance of this sort was the case of "Joe" Tinker. They say that when Tinker first came to the Big League, he was very weak as a hitter. He chopped his bat up short and stood close to the plate. Matty tells me that he was a "sucker" on a curve ball on the outside. Then "Joe" kept figuring how to overcome his weakness, which he knew as well as the pitchers, for he is a smart ball player. At last, he decided he would entirely renovate his form, so he got a great long bat and gripped it down by the handle, taking a big swing at the ball. Then he stood back from the plate, something after the fashion of Hans Wagner, whom I saw play in the 1909 world's series. Tinker would wade into the ball, and his batting improved at once. Last season he hit three hundred, and I believe it was the best year of his career.

"Jack" Barry of the Athletics was a bad hitter when he first came to the Philadelphia club, but the magician, "Connie" Mack, talked and reasoned with him, and Barry is now one of the most dangerous pinch hitters in our league. He is to be feared at any time when a hit will break up a game. But "Connie" was a wonder always at bolstering up weak hitters. He can find a fault in form and correct it quicker than any other man in baseball, I believe, and yet like many successful critics, he was never a heavy walloper himself when he was in the game. Neither was George Stallings. These two can tell others their faults, but cannot pick their own.

Of course, the greatest strain that any batter encounters, especially a man with a reputation, is when he enters the world's series. One of the finest exhibitions of hitting that I ever saw, except, of course, the work of Frank Baker, in a world's series was that of Honus Wagner when the Detroit club played Pittsburgh for the championship in 1909, and when it required seven games to settle the argument. By one of those strange freaks of baseball luck, a pitcher of whom little had been known before the series and on whose work we had done practically no figuring, stepped out in front and pitched the Tigers to death. His name was "Babe" Adams. This frequently happens in a world's series—that some unknown becomes the star, which the stars do not shine with good records.

But not so with the great German. Before the series we had received hints from the supposed wise ones in the game that Wagner would not show well in the series, that he had fallen down in 1903 in the series against Boston. Since then I have heard that Wagner's showing in his previous world's series had worried him all the following years he spent in the game until 1909, and that he had been waiting for this opportunity to vindicate himself. He certainly did it, for his batting was responsible for nearly half of the runs scored by the Pirates in that series if my memory has not altogether failed me. His style looks almost awkward to me as he stands far back from the plate with his feet apart and his elbows flapping from his sides as if he were about to fly. But he does not let any balls that he might reach get away from him. It was a splendid exhibition of nerve that he gave in 1909, and although it beat the Detroit club out of the best chance it ever had to win the big series, and although it took a lot of money away from my fellow players and me because we had to accept the losers' end of the purse instead of the winners', still nobody could help but admire the Dutchman.

Of course, Frank Baker is the ideal hitter for a world's series, because he never worries about what he is going to do. I'll admit that the strain for me is a great one, and I never have had the luck in a big series that I have during the season. Baker has done much better in his last two world's series than he did in the one when the Athletics faced and defeated the Cubs. If you will look up his record you will find that Frank did not bat so well in Chicago as he did in Philadelphia in that series. Further, if you will examine Baker's record, you will discover that he always hits better at home than on the road.

American Leaguers attribute this to two causes. One is that Frank must have his sea food diet. Strange as it may sound, he never plays as good ball when he gets so far inland that he cannot get his oysters and lobsters and crabs. He seems to go best on the food to which he is accustomed on the eastern shore of Maryland, where his home is and where he has always lived. I honestly do not think Baker would have been rated the great player he is to-day if, through the luck of baseball, he had been signed with St. Louis, say, where it is next to impossible to get fresh sea food in the summer time. It is easy to get it in Philadelphia, which is near the coast.

"What do you feed Baker during the world's series?" somebody asked "Connie" Mack last fall after he had defeated the Giants for the second time.

"That's my secret," replied "Connie," with a smile.

But all the members of the Athletics will tell you that Frank is peculiar about his food. He does not seem to be happy when he fails to get just the sort of diet he is used to, and naturally when he is unhappy he does not go so well. Nobody does.

Again, Baker is a very quiet, unassuming sort of fellow who is almost diffident off the field. He is extremely fond of his home, and spends most of the time there when he is out of his uniform. On the road, he is therefore lost for occupation and longs for the time when the club will get back home. This does not help his batting, and for that reason he never hits as well on the road. Now, if McGraw could have cornered all the sea food and held out on Baker during the past two world's series, he might have had better luck. I hope that no one will think I am not loyal to the American League for slipping this tip about Baker's gastronomic taste.

Nearly every hitter in baseball either prefers the road or home. Some go better away, while others are weaklings on the road and strong at the home grounds. Personally, I hit better when on the road, because I like the opposition of foreign crowds. They key me up and that is what I need. On the other hand, my great rival in the American League, who is more phlegmatic in his nature, busts them better at home than he does on the road. Most of my gains were made on Jackson last summer when both clubs were making long trips through the east. This condition of things is hard to explain, as are many other recognized facts in baseball.

Some clubs are better road clubs than at home. The Giants, they tell me, always bat stronger away from their own doorstep. The New York players maintained for a long time that it was the glaring, bright-hued advertising signs in center field that hurt their hitting at home. But a nice green background was painted in at the Polo Grounds for the benefit of the hitters and still they continue to be a better road club.

There is a peculiar phenomenon in connection with the Athletics and their uniforms. I hear fault found with the drab traveling uniforms of the Athletics all around the American League circuit, and, in fact, neither "Connie" Mack nor his players think that these dirty looking uniforms are worthy of being entered in an art exhibit or a tailors' show.

But for several seasons the Athletics played good ball at home, and always fell back as soon as they hit the road. They wore quite natty and pretentious uniforms for traveling purposes in those days, but perhaps they were too careful of them for fear of spoiling the cut or creases or something, for they won few ball games in them. Then Mack got the dull drab traveling uniforms for the club in 1910. They looked so bad when new that there was no chance of spoiling them. The boys got away to a fine jump on the first trip and came through with the pennant largely through the good work on the road. They have been a great road ball club ever since, hitting like demons away from home, and at home, too, for that matter. "Connie" has received many protests against the looks of the uniforms, but to all kickers he makes the same reply:

"We win ball games on the road in them. That is all we put on uniforms for. We are not representing a fashionable summer hotel, you know."

I guess he's right, too. They certainly win ball games.

Lajoie is one of the players who "bust them" whether he is on the road or at home. It does not make any difference to him, but he is one ball player who will probably never have an equal. He is just a natural hitter, and I don't look for any more ball players to have his wonderful record for continued hitting, because his smooth, easy temperament is responsible for it. He has the temperament to last. Most others have not the nervous systems to keep up the sustained pace. Lajoie never tries to outguess the pitcher. He does not need to. He even whangs at bad balls, a cardinal sin in most batters, and turns them into base hits. He kind of shuffles up to the plate in a sleepy sort of way, with a challenge to the pitcher in his swagger.

"Come on. I dare you to put one over," he says by his manner.

Lajoie has the pitcher half licked before he ever steps into the box—that is, most pitchers. They are all afraid of him, and nervousness makes it easier for him to push the pill a mile.

They tell a funny story about Lajoie and a recruit pitcher who joined a certain American League club late one season. He was green from the bushes, and no intellectual giant anyway, spending little of his time in reading the newspapers. As the race was practically settled when this youngster joined out, the manager sent him to the box against Cleveland one day for his tryout. He was getting along fairly well when Lajoie came to the bat in the fourth or fifth inning with a couple of men on the bases and two outs. Most of his own players on the bench, the fans in the stands, and even the Cleveland players began to feel almost sorry for the young pitcher, who was about to have his hopes of Big League fame blasted by a drive from the Frenchman's bat. The manager thought of taking the youngster out, but finally figured that he would let him stay in the game and absorb his medicine, because the winning or losing of the contest would make no difference in the ultimate standing of the club. The men on the pitcher's own club began to feel sorry for themselves and the third baseman moved back a few steps, as Lajoie has a bad habit of "busting them" down that alley at a rate which is liable to cut a third baseman's "bean" right loose if he is playing in too close. Then, when all these preparations had been perfected, the pitcher fanned out Lajoie, much to the surprise of the ball players and spectators. He started for the bench while the crowd shouted. He did not take off his cap, and the fans put it down to his modesty and applauded louder, because a crowd likes to see an unassuming youngster. So do ball players.

"Who is getting the big hand?" he asked the folks on the bench as he took the customary drink of water.

"It's for you because you whiffed the big Frenchman," replied the manager.

"Who is he?" inquired the recruit.

"Larry Lajoie."

The busher almost fell in a faint.

"Was that the guy I just fanned out?" gasped the startled pitcher.

"The one," said the manager.

"I feel like going and apologizing to him for it," remarked the pitcher.

If he had known who Lajoie was before the Frenchman came to the bat, he would have been licked. As a matter of fact, the historians go further with the story and declare that the next time "Larry" faced the young twirler he did not know whether he was pitching baseball or not and that Lajoie hit the ball a mile. This does not sound likely, since the great tendency in baseball is for a pitcher who gets away in good shape against a big star to believe that he has something on that man always and to pitch well against him, even if poor batters make this same twirler look like a dub. However, Lajoie is not of the temperament to admit that any pitcher has anything on him.

There is another old story about Lajoie which is so old that perhaps it may listen new by now. Several seasons back, Sheridan, the veteran umpire of the American League, was working a game alone, and so he was getting the balls and strikes from behind the pitcher's box, since there were some runners on the bases at the time this incident occurred, and he might be called upon to make a decision in the infield. A busher was pitching the contest, in which Cleveland was one of the clubs, when the great Lajoie strode up to the bat. This youngster, who knew the Frenchman both by sight and reputation, turned to the umpire and asked:

"What's his groove?"

"A straight one right over the middle of the plate," replied Sheridan, "and then you lie down flat on your stomach if you don't want them to call the hearse. I'll be flat behind you, never fear."

Lajoie, as I have been trying to point out and illustrate with anecdotes, is not the type of batter who endeavors to outguess a pitcher, but he is one of the few free-swingers in baseball who can get away with this style. A man has to be a natural hitter to be a free-swinger. I do not consider myself a natural hitter. There are not more than ten in both Big Leagues at present, I believe. Sherwood Magee of the Philadelphia club in the National League, they tell me, is one. I have never seen him play. Lajoie is one. The great Delehanty used to be one. There are players who can hold their bats away down at the end and back on their shoulders and take the long wallop at the ball, because they have naturally remarkable eyes and are wonderful judges of distance and speed.

But the ordinary stars of the game are the men who choke their bats up short and use their wits. Speaker and Collins are of this type. They always observe closely where the infielders are playing and perhaps try to draw the third baseman in a little with a bluff as if to bunt, so that they can break one down past him. There are a hundred tricks which can be applied when one is at the plate if a man is concentrating on his work and has his wits about him. I believe it is due to constant figuring that I have been able to hit. Whenever I go to the box, I try to outguess the pitcher and get him in the hole. Some twirlers will look at a hitter's feet, believing, perhaps, that in this way they can get a line on where he intends to try to place the ball. Often, I make a bluff that I mean to hit to right field, when my real plan is to get one past the third baseman, who, I notice out of the tail of my eye, is playing away from the bag a foot too far. The pitcher guesses my bluff, as I intend him to, and serves me a ball on the outside which would be very difficult for a left-handed hitter to pull to right. It is just the sort I am looking for, and I get my chance to "bust" it over third base.

"I'm kissing them all on a line, but right into somebody's hands,"

I frequently hear batters complain. "Gee, I can't get any breaks in the luck."

If a man finds that he is doing this, he should examine his own style, and he will generally find that there is something wrong with it. He, himself, is usually to blame for this kind of luck. Perhaps his feet are too close together or too far apart. Maybe he is swinging too hard in an effort to be a hard hitter. The most foolish thing any batter can try to do is to attempt to drive the ball over the fence or "press." This has hurt many a promising batter. It looked to be the fault with the Giants' hitting in both series against the Athletics that I saw. They are naturally a club of short-swingers and chop-hitters. They all choke their bats short, but against Philadelphia they were all so anxious to compile wonderful records that they forgot their true form and were taking the big wallop and missing the ball by a foot in most cases. I believe it was this fault which made them look so bad as hitters in these series. McGraw admitted it one night in 1911 when we were in a hotel discussing the series during the long rainy spell when the Giants were tied up in Philadelphia.

"My players have tried to become sluggers and free-swingers overnight," complained McGraw, "and I can't get them to stop taking the big wallop at the ball. That is what has hurt their hitting. They refuse to chop it."

Before the season was over last year, Frank Chance, by his coaching, did a lot to improve the batting of several men on the New York American League Club who had cardinal faults in form. A player should be able to hit to any field at all if he puts his feet right. We in the American League all realize that "Birdie" Cree of the Yankees was a natural right-field hitter. Almost any time he got one it went to right, but this fact did not become generally well known in the league during Cree's first season, and therefore he was rated as a great slugger. He didn't look so good afterwards, because all the right fielders played for him. No other New York manager thought to correct this fault in Cree until Chance came along.

"You don't place your feet right," advised Chance. "You'll hit to right as long as you stand that way."

"Can't change my form now," replied Cree, "and I've been doing pretty well with this style."

"Not well enough to suit me," answered Chance. "And you'll change your form or change your job."

Cree preferred to change his form, and toward the end of last season he was hitting to all the fields. Members of the Yankees tell me that Chance is a great driver. It will probably be recalled that he batted twice as a pinch hitter in a game against the St. Louis Browns one day last summer and got away with it. The umpire has no right to stop a man doing this unless the opposing club protests, and the Browns were not in the game enough to notice it. I don't believe Chance could have put this over against any other team in the league, because the players on the other clubs are at least alert.

The Yankees' manager went to bat for a pitcher and then he walked up to the plate in the excitement of a long rally to hit for a regular player whose turn it was, as I recall the incident from reading of it in the newspapers.

"What would you have done if the Browns had protested and you had not gotten away with it?" somebody asked Chance later.

"I would have walked right back to the bench and risked my good right hand by busting that wooden head in the nose and then released him," replied Chance. "I don't want any man on my club who has so little ambition that he cannot remember when it is his turn to bat, and who will let me go to the plate in his turn without making a protest."

It is needless to add that a player of this type and with this sort of interest in the game never makes a three-hundred hitter. The man in question is now back in the minors.

As a rule, one of the hardest styles of delivery for any hitter to connect with is the spitball, because it generally breaks very sharply. Therefore, teams are always watching this sort of pitcher for some sign to show when he is going to throw a spitter. I mentioned the fact in a preceding article that Frank Smith, once with the White Sox, would always look at the ball when he put it up to his mouth to wet it and really intended to let go a spitter. If he were only bluffing, he would not look at it. Nearly every team in the league got on to this and banged him all over the lot before he found out how they were doing it.

The Athletics once discovered that "Ed" Walsh raised his eyebrows when he really wet the ball to pitch a spitter, and this made the peak of his cap go up and down. If he were only bluffing, the peak of his cap was stationary. They hit him on account of this information until somebody tipped Walsh off. But the batters who are always looking for the little things like that and who are alert are the ones finishing up in the three-hundred set. They are always trying to get something on the pitcher, and generally do. The pitcher usually has something on the sleepy ones.

And in hitting a man needs bunches of self-confidence. If he is inclined to step away from a curve ball, let him draw a line when practicing from the back of the heel of his front foot parallel to the plate, and make up his mind not to step over this. A man can frequently break himself of stepping back by putting his feet farther apart for the time being. It is best to keep the feet close together when in position ordinarily, I believe, but I have seen players broken of being "bat shy" by spreading the feet a little. Some men can be cured by permitting themselves to get hit by a pitched ball once or twice, so that they may know it does not hurt much. It is hardly felt when an athlete in training gets a blow in the body if he tightens up his muscles.

But, most important, don't ever let the pitcher think he has anything on you.

CHAPTER X

Tragedies of
the Diamond

There comes a time in the career of every Big Leaguer when he begins to get old, and he starts going back. Others are cut down at the tops of their careers through accidents in games. Whenever a ball player goes into a contest, he runs the chance of ending his career. What happened to John Coombs and "Wild Bill" Donovan, and others. The tragedy of the "busher" whom "Bill" Bradley threatened to "get," and how he "got" him.

Many tragedies of the diamond are written down in the history of the Big Leagues every season. Ball players will fight for their Big League lives as hard as the ordinary man struggles against the call of the undertaker. Nearly all stars realize it when they begin to fade, but not a few successfully conceal the fact from their managers for some time by shrewdness in covering up their increasing weaknesses, such as slowness in the field or weak throwing arms.

But the real tragedies of the diamond center about the men who are cut down in their prime. Every time a player enters a game of ball he is taking a chance on being injured in such a way that he may never again be able to appear in uniform. This is one of the risks of the profession which cannot be avoided.

"Danny" Murphy was a star with the Athletics in 1911, and it was his fine work and shrewd field leadership—for he was the captain of the club then—that had much to do with the Philadelphia team taking the championship of the American League, and finally the supreme title of champions of the world. He got away in good shape in the following season and, although a veteran, played great ball, until one day he hurt his knee. He thought little of the damage at the time and broke back into the game before the knee was as solid as once it had been. The Athletics sorely needed him, for the club was not going well, and, as will be remembered, Boston finally beat them out.

"Danny" hadn't been back in the battle long before the knee started to give him trouble once more, and I picked up a morning paper one day and read the statement that "Danny" Murphy had water on the knee. It was nursed along and cared for by the best specialists of the country, but it refused to mend. Murphy has never appeared regularly in the Philadelphia lineup since then, and hardly a day has passed that "Danny" does not grieve.

"I wish I had my leg again, 'Ty,'" he told me one day last spring when Detroit was playing the Athletics. "If I was right below the waist line, I know I would have several more years of good baseball left in me."

"Connie" Mack has carried Murphy for two seasons, perhaps partly for the sake of his judgment and advice in running the club, but probably more for sentimental reasons. It was only a few days ago that I read in the newspaper that Murphy would probably be released this year. It will be a real tragedy of the diamond when "Danny" passes out, and I know "Connie" Mack will hate to let him go, because he takes good care of the men who have served him well, and Murphy has done well by the Athletics.

"I don't know what I'll do when they get through with me in the Big League," said "Danny" one day. "Baseball has always been my life."

And there is John Coombs, also of the Athletics. Coombs is one of the really great pitchers of the day, or was, because of wonderful speed, a grand curve ball, apparently inexhaustible strength, and a "heart" of tempered steel. Probably his "heart" or courage was his greatest asset, for no pinch was ever too tough for him to face and usually master. He practically pitched the Athletics to their first world's championship in 1910, when that club beat the Cubs, and he showed just as good form against the Giants in 1911, until the accident occurred which really has been responsible for keeping him out of baseball ever since. It was also one of those quick diamond casualties which occur so often in baseball.

The Giants had won only a single game in the 1911 series and the Athletics had three to their credit when John Coombs started out to work in the fifth contest in New York. He was the Coombs of iron through six innings, but in the seventh he strained himself in fielding a sharply-hit ball to the pitcher's box. Even the watchful "Connie" Mack on the bench did not notice the twinge in Coombs' face as the pain shot through him. But I was following the game from the press stand and happened to be placed right behind the catcher. All at once Coombs seemed to slow up. He was not the same.

"Something is wrong with John," I said to the man sitting next to me.

Hardly had I made the remark than the batter cracked out a hit. I do not recall who this was. The Giants soon discovered that the man working in the box for the Athletics was not the same who had mowed them down through the early innings. The Athletics knew it, too, and the smiles of victory which had been spreading on their faces inning by inning were displaced by grave looks. "Connie" did not have another pitcher warmed up, because Coombs had been moving so steadily to what looked like certain victory through the opening rounds that the precaution did not seem necessary. The men on the Philadelphia club were worried and began to stall and look to the bench. Collins stopped the game while he walked to the pitcher's box and picked up an imaginary pebble. Meanwhile, he talked to Coombs. It could be observed from the press stand that the players were making anxious inquiry of one another about Coombs, for they were constantly putting their gloves to their mouths and talking behind them. You could tell that they were saying questioningly, anxiously:

"What's the matter with John?"

An emissary from the bench further delayed the game while he conferred with Thomas, the Philadelphia catcher, and Ira walked to Coombs. John shook his head, and Thomas in turn shook his head at the bench. Of course, Mack knew that something was wrong with his pitcher, but he did not want to ask Coombs to quit under fire. He has said since that he would rather have lost the game than to have taken John out against his will. And all the time while the game went on the pain, with the intensity of a toothache, was shooting through Coombs with his every move.

"I expected it would stop, that it was only a temporary strain," John has told me since. "And I wanted to stick that game out and be in on the final victory of the Athletics if I could."

The Giants, knowing that something was wrong with Coombs, went after him with the grim spirit of despair and the inspiration of a fighting chance. They began to cut down the lead of the Athletics. Mack had another pitcher warming up by this time, and finally the side was retired. There was a between-innings conference on the Philadelphia bench, and "Connie" decided to let John go on, believing that he could hold his lead through the two remaining innings.

He did not realize the extent of the injury, for Coombs, after his way, made light of it.

So Coombs went back to work in the eighth, and the Athletics were still ahead when the inning was over, but the Giants were closing up on them and hitting John. The pain was worse in the ninth, and the players on the Philadelphia club had to stall often. John could not conceal the agony he was suffering, but he pitched grimly on. In the last gasp of the ninth the score was tied, and Coombs was done. Another pitcher finished the game for Philadelphia, and the Athletics lost. That night John Coombs was in a hospital in Philadelphia and was pitching the final innings of the game over, so his nurses have said. They had to hold him down in his bed because he got the notion that someone was trying to take him out of the box, and he was fighting against it.

Coombs was never right in 1912. He came back for the season of 1913 after a winter on his farm in Maine, and he declared it would be his best year. But members of the Philadelphia club have told me since that John was listless throughout the training season and did not display the "pep" to which they were accustomed in the man. "Connie" Mack sent him against Boston in the first game of the season, and the flush on his cheek made Mack believe that John was right again. "Connie" knows now that it was the fever flush. Let John relate this chapter in his own words as he told it to me after he joined his club for a short time late in the summer of 1913 after his long siege of illness. Said John:

"As I warmed up for that opening battle against Boston I never felt more fit in my life. I had lots of stuff and wanted to work, because I seemed strong. It was the false strength of fever. This lasted through the early innings, and then I began to feel dizzy, and black specks started up before my eyes, and the batters became indistinct. My curve would not break.

"'What's the matter, John?' 'Connie' asked me.

"'I'm not right,' I replied, and 'Connie' took me out."

That night John Coombs had a temperature of 104, and it required only a couple of days for the physicians to confirm their belief that it was typhoid. The old strain of the 1911 world's series had gotten one of the gamest pitchers of the diamond. Somewhere in the South, Coombs had encountered the typhoid germ. Doubtless this same enemy of society had found its way into the systems of the other members of the Athletics. But their good physical condition made it possible for them to throw it off. In John it found a good lodging place, for the old strain which had put him in the hospital had weakened him.

It was weeks before Coombs was out of bed, and there were times when those in charge had grave doubts whether he would ever get up again. Big Leaguers on all the clubs asked about John solicitously, for his type is popular in the profession. At last he was able to sit up and then walk around a little. The danger from typhoid was past.

John then set about it grimly to recover his health and strength. He went to the Maine woods and lived in the open. When it looked certain toward the end of summer that his club would once more be a contender in the world's series, he wrote "Connie" Mack that he felt strong enough to join the team, and that he expected, with six weeks of work, to be in shape to take his turn in the box during the world's series. He concluded by saying he did not feel that he should draw salary all season and share in the world's series' money without getting a chance to do some work. Mack was doubtful and wrote back, asking Coombs whether he was sure he was strong enough to begin to work out with the club again. John replied that there was no doubt about it.

For a time it seemed as if the great pitcher had been correct in his opinion about his strength, for he took easy workouts and appeared to possess all his old ability. I saw him shortly after he had rejoined his club.

"How do you feel, John?" I asked him, after shaking hands and telling him how glad I was to see him back in uniform.

"Fine from the waist up," he answered. "My legs are still a little weak from being in bed so long."

"You look heavier, John, than the last time I saw you," I told Coombs, and he did.

Coombs took his daily workouts, going a little bit harder each day, until it looked as if he would surely be able to make good on his promise to "Connie" to pitch in the series.

"Coombs is going to be right for the series," Evans, the umpire, told me several weeks after John had reported. I had not seen Coombs for some time myself then and was asking about his progress.

Then, one morning, I picked up the newspaper and saw that the Iron Man of the Athletics was back in the hospital because he had overdone things again. The world's series had been long played and won when Coombs was again able to leave the hospital. And he was a fraction of an inch shorter in his height this time. When he once more went to his Maine farm he stoutly declared he would yet be pitching for the Athletics, and as good as ever. That was his dauntless courage asserting itself again. And if any man can make it, John Coombs can, because he has a heart of iron. But I doubt if he ever pitches again. And so John Coombs' career furnishes another real tragedy of the diamond.

It seems as though the Athletics have had some of the best and worst luck in our league. The consistent winning of championships has meant money to the club and players, but there is still another tragedy of the club that comes to my mind. It was not very many years ago that there was a catcher on the team with all the earmarks of a coming star. His name was "Doc" Powers, and he was a popular man not only with the players on his own club, but with those on the opposing teams of the league. While still a young man and in his baseball prime, he was cut down. His death put the team in mourning and took the spirit out of several of the players for some time. They played ball in a hang-dog sort of way.

Although the Athletics appear to have been the biggest sufferers in our league in this respect, all teams have their tragedies. Few fans realize that "Bill" Donovan, once the star with the Detroit club, and now the manager of a minor league team, that of Providence, pitched the last two years he was with the Tigers with his arm paining him every time he made a move to throw the ball. "Wild Bill" would wince with each delivery toward the end of a hard game in those days, yet he had more stuff than ever.

"Bill" hurt the wing one day, and it never came back to its true shape. Still, he did not admit its condition to Jennings or any of the players on the team until he could no longer conceal his suffering from the watchful gaze of Jennings. Then he made light of the injury.

"It's never been right," he told Jennings, "since I pitched it out that day, but I guess a little work will put it right."

The "little work" did not fix it, but Donovan stayed in fast company for two years with the arm aching him like a toothache, and I never heard him murmur or try to dodge an assignment to pitch on the plea that his wing was in no condition to work. Finally, he had to give up and his heart ached him worse than his arm then.

Of course, there are countless tragedies in the spring when the batches of recruits join Big League clubs with their hopes high that they will make good and stick in the majors. Then there are the veterans who wear out in the service and get old and still struggle on, making the fight to last a few years longer in the "spangles." When a youngster goes South in the spring to join the Big Leaguers, he generally has pictured himself in the uniform of the club while thousands cheer his good playing. I know I had my dreams before my trial. Then comes the weeding-out process, when the disappointed candidates are sent back to the minors one by one, some for good and others for more seasoning. I believe I have seen more tragedies around a spring training camp than anywhere else in the world. What hurts is for these boys to go back home and admit that they could not make good after having had the big chance.

Some recruits show slowly, while others endeavor to start out with a rush. It is this over-ambition which sends so many back, because a youngster is liable to hurt himself for the season by overworking before the winter stiffness and staleness is out of his muscles. This is particularly true of the young pitchers, who are invariably so eager to show that some of them endeavor to curve a ball on the first day, and generally show up on the second with a lame arm and are never fit to perform again before the team leaves for the North. They are sent back to the minors, therefore, practically without a trial, because a manager cannot afford to spend too much time or to be too discriminating in the hustle and bustle of spring practice.

It is not well known that the White Sox almost let "Reb" Russell, one of the great pitching finds of 1913, go back to the "bushes." Russell was a wise youngster and did not hurry his conditioning in the California camp, where the White Sox train, and run risks of a lame wing. His work was so mediocre by the time the team broke camp that five or six young pitchers looked more promising to Callahan, and "Reb" was sent along with the second team, Callahan not deeming it worth his while to watch Russell closely any more, because of the little he had shown.

But "Jimmie" heard glowing reports of the pitching of this youth as the second team of the White Sox worked it way home, and he decided when the club got back to Chicago that he would hold on to "Reb" and see if he showed anything.

The first time I saw Russell in the box he looked very bad, and had all the habits a young pitcher should not have, but he carried plenty of nerve. He used a motion toward first base to hold up runners which was easily a balk.

I recall the first game the Detroit team played with him pitching. He gave me a base on balls, and had evidently been told to watch me to see that I did not get too big a lead off the bag. The first thing I knew, bang! he had shot the ball to first base after having made a very perceptible motion toward the batter which was plainly a balk. Of course, he had me easily, so I broke for second, there being nothing much else to do. As luck would have it, I got into the bag safely anyway, but I thought it was time to protest on the motion.

"What do you call that, 'Billy'?" I asked Evans, who was umpiring the game.

"What do you call it, 'Ty'?" he asked.

"A balk, if I ever saw one," I replied promptly.

"You're right, but you were safe, anyway," answered Evans, "so what is the use of scaring the youngster to death? I'll warn him. You could not advance further than second base on the balk."

Evans gave Russell a word of warning, and instead of it flustering him, he at once set to work to correct the faulty move to the bag and now has as good a one as any twirler in the league, except such experts in this line as "Ed" Walsh and some of those others with the great and studied move to the bag that just shades being a balk, but which is not, according to the rules. Russell is a splendid example of the wise recruit, while the five or six other young twirlers who were supposed to be better and who traveled back from the camp with the first team of the White Sox are still sticking in the minors.

X. Tragedies of the Diamond

We had a young pitcher come South to join the Detroit club a few seasons ago who looked like another Walter Johnson. He had worlds of speed and a fine break on his curve ball. Jennings, as usual, warned all his pitchers against going at it hard until they had worked out well, but on the third day after the regulars reached camp this youngster was sent to the box to pitch to the batters for hitting practice. None of the boys was batting much, and when it came my turn I was surprised to see one come up with a big hook on it that missed my bat a foot or so. Of course, I could not do anything much against curve-ball pitching with all the winter's dust on my lamps, and so I struck out. The boy grinned all over. He was sure he was making good. I hunted up Jennings, who was coaching some of the recruits in the art of the fall-away slide.

"Say, 'Hughie,'" said I, "that youngster out there is throwing hooks and putting on steam as if it was the middle of August."

"I didn't think you fellows were hitting them much," said Jennings. "Hey, you!" he yelled at the young pitcher. "Come here."

The recruit shot up one more fast one and then, still grinning, ambled over to the manager.

"What are you trying to do?" bawled Jennings. "Didn't I tell you to take it easy? Go back to the hotel and see if the trainer can keep that wing of yours from dropping off after the way you have used it."

The boy, expecting praise instead of blame, hung his head and went. The trainer could not do anything for the arm, and it was so sore during the rest of our stay in the spring camp that he was not fit to show again. He went back to the minors after coming up to the training camp with high hopes. He is in the "bushes" yet. And I'll lay ten to one that he still tells back home that they turned him out after he had fanned most of the Detroit sluggers.

"You've got to have a pull to break into the Big League," he doubtless concludes his story. I know, because I have heard many of them talk.

A young pitcher named "Tom" Hanley went South with the Giants one spring and he looked good during the brief chance he got to show. Newspaper men who were on the Giants' training trip have told me that he was extremely ambitious and kept writing letters home to his wife telling her how he was going to make good among the Big Fellows and that better days were due for the Hanley family. One morning Hanley did not leave his room, and a few days later he was dead. All his Big League ambitions had faded in his sudden end in the training camp before he ever had an opportunity to show. Death on a ball team is always very depressing to the players. Members of the Giants tell me that they could not get out of Marlin soon enough after Hanley's death.

"It hung crape on the whole camp," Mathewson said.

The Giants have had their share of tragedies. McGraw dug up a very promising left-hander in the South in 1911 named "Dave" Robertson. I know he would have made good in the Big League, because I am familiar with his record. He is one of those men who are born athletes, and who have the knack of doing anything in this line well. Besides being a great college pitcher, he was the star football player at the University of Virginia. When McGraw signed this boy he said to him:

"Now I want you to promise me not to play football next fall."

Robertson still had another year to finish his college course, and he planned to do this before joining the Giants. The boy promised, but when the snappy days of the fall came around and he felt that his college needed his services, he forgot his promise to the Giants' manager, and went into the game. He quit it when they broke his collar bone, and this accident stripped his pitching arm of its power. A brilliant Big League career was undoubtedly spoiled for this youngster simply because he entered one game of football. All predicted that he was one of the coming left-handers of the game, and good southpaws are scarce enough. Now McGraw thinks he has turned him into an outfielder; he put him out with a minor league club in 1913, with instructions to the manager to try him in the outer pasture. This manager returned Robertson, with glowing accounts of his hitting and fielding ability. But he will never shine as an outfielder as he would have shone as a star southpaw if he had kept his promise. Therefore, the blighting of his career as a pitcher before he even got into the Big League was a tragedy.

There is the story of a busher on the St. Louis Browns who was particularly fresh and who got into a row with "Bill" Bradley, the old third baseman of the Cleveland club, one day because he was a little careless about exposing his spikes as he slid into the base. "Bill" said it was only due to his own shiftiness that he avoided being cut.

"I'll get you for that, young fellow," said "Bill" to the boy.

The first chance Bradley had he cut into the recruit with his spikes.

"How do you like that kind of sliding?" said "Bill."

The boy only laughed.

"You cut my uniform a little," he said. Then he finished the game.

It was noticed that he dropped out of the league after that contest, but none thought of it until late the next season. Many "bushers" come and go. Then "Bill" got a note on the bench one day asking him to step over to a certain part of the stand. There sat a young fellow with a beard of a week on his face and his clothes in tatters.

"Who are you?" asked Bradley.

"Remember the young fellow with the St. Louis club you said you'd get?" asked the young fellow. "Well, I'm that guy. You got me, all right."

"I remember you now, but I didn't even know you were cut," answered "Bill." "You finished the game."

"Certainly I finished the game," said the other. "Did you think I was going to lay down? That was when the bone in my leg got infected. Dirt got into the cut. Haven't been able to use the leg since."

Bradley told the boy to come to the clubhouse after the contest, and "Bill" dug down in the old sock.

"Gee, I'm sorry," remarked Bradley thoughtfully as he dressed. "That boy looked like a comer, too."

The passing of the old boys is a tragedy. We all always hate to see a veteran go. The releasing of a man who has done good work for a club is one of the hardest of tasks for most managers. The dissolution of that old and famous machine, Chance's Cubs, was a combination tragedy. Mordecai Brown, the grand pitcher, who had done as much as any one player to make him his fortune, Murphy let go without even permitting the three-fingered wonder to share in the gains of a post-season series with the White Sox after his last season with the club. Chance was kicked out, too. And then outsiders blame ball players for holding out and kicking for all the money they can get while the going is good. We never know what day we will be cut down with a spike or be turned out because the period of usefulness has passed.

A few years ago when the Pirates were playing on the campground of the old Sportsmen's Park in Pittsburgh, Honus Wagner was all crippled up with rheumatism in his legs, and it was feared that he was nearing the end of his career. But he played gamely and steadily on with never a murmur, standing out there on that wet ground with pains in his legs that shot up to his eye teeth every time he moved. Some baseball people say that the moving of the Pirate Park to the higher ground, the present Forbes Field, was made in the hope that it would add some seasons to Wagner's baseball life.

It apparently has, for the big Dutchman is certainly going yet. But his case was almost a tragedy.

So it will be seen that the profession of baseball might come under the head of "hazardous occupations." I believe I can truthfully say that no man in the Big League intentionally cuts another for the sake of putting him out of the game. The common motto is live and let live. But none of us ever enters a contest without running the chance that it may snuff out our career.

But the great overwhelming tragedy comes when a star is humiliated by being forced back into the minors. Many of the men of the game now save their money in order to be able to retire at the finish of their major league days. As I said in a previous article, I hope to quit the game when I am thirty. They will never get me into the minors. Perhaps I may quit sooner if I am cut down some day and hurt so bad that none of the bonesetters can put me right again. "Bonesetter" Reese of Youngstown, Ohio, has saved many a pitcher's arm. Some managers have even contemplated sending players to him to have their heads treated. But he can't save the boys whose futures are behind them.

CHAPTER XI

Is Baseball a
Good Profession?

*Why it is hard to make good in the Big League, and what it means
to a man financially and otherwise if he becomes a star. The improvement of the class of men in baseball in the last few years, and the
manner in which they live. A study of the personalities of some of
the players and what they have accomplished for themselves. It is a
fine profession when a man makes good in it like any other. What
it has done for me.*

McGraw once said to me when I was discussing the subject of
baseball as a profession with the Giants' leader:

"If I ever had had a son, I would like to have seen him a ball
player, because I think it is a good business. It keeps a man healthy
in both mind and body, and it pays a young fellow more when he
starts than almost any business he could break into."

I don't know that I would go so far as McGraw in desiring that
a son of mine should play Big League ball, but then I have a son and
"Mac" hasn't. However, I will go this far. I will say that baseball has
been a good profession to me. But, like most fathers, I am not particularly anxious that my son should follow in my footsteps.

My father was no exception to the rule—he kicked worse than Clarke
Griffith does on a close play called against him.

Perhaps the reason for this is that I know how hard it is to make good in the Big League, and how big a percentage there is against a boy becoming a star. Anybody can see this when he stops to think that there are thousands of ball players in this country and room for only about four hundred among the top-notchers. The entrance of the Federal League into baseball will not increase the number of Big League players by more than two hundred. And I know that there are just as good men in the bushes and small towns as there are in the Big Leagues to-day, but they have never been discovered and therefore have never had a chance to make good. Scouts and managers tell you that they cannot get good players—that there aren't any more left of Big League caliber. The trouble is not that they do not exist, but that they cannot be found.

After a player has made good in the Big League and established his position in fast company, however, I believe that baseball is one of the best professions there is right now, not only because of the money in it, but for other reasons. Scatter your eye over the men in the majors to-day, and you will find players living well and driving automobiles who would be working in coal mines or cotton mills or at some other very unremunerative trade if they had not possessed the ability to play ball and the opening had not been offered them. People will tell you that baseball leads to nothing, and that, after perhaps ten years of service, when he is no longer fast enough for the Big Leagues, a man has not builded anything for the future. They point to the finishes of such players as "Bugs" Raymond and "Rube" Waddell, Raymond dying broke, while "Rube," without funds, is at present so ill that he is liable to die any day and is completely down and out. There are no more "Bugs" Raymonds and "Rube" Waddells in the business now, because there is no room for them, and it won't be long before you will have heard of the last benefit being given for an old and broken-down Big Leaguer who was a good fellow when he had it. Ball players are making a profession out of the game. In the days of the "bad actors," it was regarded by the players as a sport and a pleasant way to spend their time.

In contrast to Raymond and Waddell, take Plank, of the Athletics, and Mathewson, of the Giants, who were really contemporaries of the other pair, but who have taken advantage of their opportunities and care of themselves and are still doing good service for their respective teams. If you look back through the history of baseball, you will find that Plank and Mathewson were among the first to take baseball seriously and to look to the future. Neither one of these will need a benefit when he hangs up his uniform for the last time, nor will he lack for a remunerative occupation. Steady stars of this sort would have been good at almost any business they had turned their hands to. "Eddie" Plank has shown that he is a good farmer, as well as pitcher, in the very fine place he has at Gettysburg, Pa., while Matty is busy with many interests outside of baseball. The influence of these two men in changing the views of players generally toward the profession and improving the position of the ball players has been very extensive, according to my notions.

But let us take a look at baseball as a profession from the point of view of the man just horning into the Big League. As I have said, once a player makes good in the majors, it is a great profession. No costly preparation is required for the game. Nearly all the big figures in baseball to-day have been poor boys without finished educations. "Connie" Mack deserted the job of a hand in a shoe factory to take up baseball. He risked a lot when he made the change, and admits it himself, but declares that he put the move up to his mother, and she approved. John McGraw was a news "butch" on trains up near where he was born in Truxton, N.Y. By "butch" I mean a newsboy who sells papers, candy, etc., but they tell me John used to engage in a little baseball while laying over between trips, until finally he got a chance as a pitcher with the Wellesville team. A college education is not necessary for a ball player to be successful, although many college men are coming into the Big League every year, and I think they have done the profession good. They generally make good players, too, if they have any natural ability, because they have been taught to think.

Even I recall the days when there existed among the old-timers a prejudice against the college boy who tried to break into the Big League. He was generally regarded as an invader by the type that was in baseball ten or fifteen years ago, and the treatment he received was none too kind, as a rule. Here is an example of what happened to many a college player when he tried to get into the game ten or twelve years ago.

A pitcher who is one of the big stars of the game now was pitching for a little minor league team up in Massachusetts several years ago, and the way the bushers were rapping his delivery did not hint that some day he was to be regarded as perhaps the greatest that ever lived. Every man who came up to the plate would take a crack at the ball, and they were all hitting at the straight ones and letting the curve balls go by with no more attention being paid to them than perhaps to spit at them in disgust. This pitcher noticed his catcher, who was an old-timer, mumbling in his mask. After seeing one batsman shake his head yes, he got an idea, did not obey the signs that the catcher gave him, pitched a curve when asked for a straight one, etc. This naturally drew a roar out of the catcher, after it had occurred two or three times, and he walked out to the pitcher's box to complain.

"What are you trying to do—cross me up?" he grumbled to the young twirler. "I just signed you for a fast one, and you served a curve."

"It is the first ball that a batter has swung at and missed in a long time," replied the pitcher. "Are you trying to cross me up by tipping off the batters to the fast balls and letting them pass up the curves?"

The catcher later admitted that he had been double-crossing the young pitcher, but did not seem to regard it as any great crime. He said his purpose in doing this was twofold. He did not think college players should be breaking into the leagues and taking the jobs away from men who could do nothing but play baseball, and he feared that, if the young pitcher made good, he would run off the team an old-timer who was tottering on his last baseball legs. This veteran was a particular pal of the catcher, and he did not care to see him go. The club could not afford to carry the youngster and the veteran, too, so the catcher was endeavoring to save the job of his pal. By tipping off the batsmen, he was getting along pretty well at it until the pitcher found him out.

In baseball there is a premium on youth, because youth means more speed, a better eye, and all the courage in the world, as a rule. Therefore, a twenty-year-old boy can be taking down just as big money in the major leagues as a thirty-year-old veteran if he can show and deliver the goods. Perhaps this statement is exaggerated a little, but many young men are drawing as big pay in baseball as the older ones, and some even bigger. A boy can start in baseball when he is eighteen or nineteen years old. In most other businesses, as a rule, no position of responsibility is given a man until he is thirty.

Take my own case. I was brought up in the little country town of Royston, Ga., and did not think when I played ball with the other boys around the lots that I was preparing for what was to be my real life work. Few players who finally reach the Big Leagues realize this, and neither do their parents, who, as a rule, object strongly when a boy proposes to go into professional baseball. This parental objection, however, is not as prevalent now as it was ten years ago. My father was no exception to this rule, and he kicked worse than Clarke Griffith does on a close play called against him when I told him I had a chance to go with the Augusta club.

"You won't be galivanting around the country playing ball," said he, "but you'll go along to school and then, when you finish there, do some real work."

After a long argument, I finally induced him to let me try it for one season. I was seventeen when I went with Augusta, and, after two days of the season, they canned me. By this time my father had taken more kindly to the idea of me playing, because he had seen some good notices about my work in the Augusta papers during the practice period, and especially after I got a double and a home run in the opening game of the season. I have found out since that he made it his duty to journey in from Royston and watch that first game of ball of the 1904 season in Augusta, although he did not tell me he was among those present until some time afterwards. When Struthers, the Augusta manager, released me because he declared I was not fast enough, my father was sore. He was never one to quit, and he would not let his son.

"So long as you are in it now, you've got to stick long enough to show them that they were wrong, Tyrus," he said. I am still sticking in my effort to convince.

"Where can you play now?" he asked me.

I told him I had an offer to go to Anniston in the Tennessee-Alabama League for very much less money.

"You'd better take it, my boy," he decided, and I did.

The next season I was in the Big League at the age of eighteen. So it will be seen that I got my chance to start at an early age, even for a ball player, and by the time I was twenty I was making good money.

XI. Is Baseball a Good Profession?

If a boy begins in the Big League before he is twenty, he has several seasons ahead when he can draw a good salary for working only about six months each year at baseball. During the off season there is an opportunity for him to establish some other business into which he can retire after he wears out as a Big Leaguer. The theoretical life of a Big League ball player is ten years, but many last longer than that now by taking good care of themselves and conserving their natural resources. This is Mathewson's fourteenth season, and pitching is supposed to wear out a man quicker than any other form of baseball work. But the great twirler of the Giants has taken wonderful care of himself, and has studied the game to discover the best methods to make himself last. If a man can spend ten years in the Big League, he should have laid away enough at the end of that time to be in a comfortable position, unless, of course, he has been unfortunate in investments. "Johnny" Evers, once the manager of the Cubs, had all the money he got out of baseball up to a few years ago in a couple of shoe stores, and he went broke on these. John had to begin all over again, practically in the middle of his career, but he was making out pretty well at the last reports I saw in the newspapers.

To devote a little more space to the cash end of the baseball business, it is a profession in which the money is always there on the first and fifteenth of each month. In other words, it is a business where you can get the ready cash without any trouble, and they do pay good salaries, especially since the Federal League started to try to drill its way into popularity with the fans.

Aside from the cash consideration, there are numerous others that make the life of a ball player an attractive one, although I will admit that the good money is its strongest boost with most of us who are in the game. However, a well-known ball player gets to meet many prominent persons who would not care to see him if he were in another profession. These people are fans and want to know the men who make baseball possible. Since I have been in the game I have met two Presidents of the United States. Mr. Taft is a great fan and used to come to the ball games in Washington frequently when he was President. President Wilson is also a follower of the Big Leagues, although I do not think he takes as keen an interest in the game or is as ardent a fan as his predecessor was. President Wilson invited me to come to the White House to see him during the 1913 season, when the Detroit club was playing a series in Washington, and he could not have treated me better if I had been a visiting prince.

"Baseball is a great game," he remarked. "Sometimes I wish I had gone into it. There are more worries attached to this job I'm holding now."

"Yes," said I, "but don't think there aren't any worries going with a job on a Big League club when you are up there fighting for a pennant."

"You're right," he replied. "It's worry that makes us ambitious and hustle. A little judicious worrying never hurt anyone."

Besides President Wilson I have met many statesmen and other prominent folks, and the memory of these meetings will stick with me long after these prominent people and the fans in general have forgotten who I am. I was introduced to the late James S. Sherman, when he was vice-president, and he was a real fan. He could tell you your batting average right off-hand and would sit down and fan with you by the hour.

Look at the wonderful opportunity that the ball players who made the trip around the world with McGraw and Comiskey had to add to their educations. This trip in itself was a great educational opportunity, because they saw many countries and people and they were learning directly from the book of life. How many of these men who made the jaunt do you suppose would have ever girdled the globe if they had not been ball players? Mr. Comiskey, John McGraw, and "Jimmie" Callahan were considered so important by the King of England that he attended the game played in London and was introduced to Mr. Comiskey and the managers of the teams. Many a society aspirant would give ten years of her life for the same opportunity, and, if the opportunity did come, weeks would be spent in preparing for the event and figuring out what to say for the royal ears to field. Comiskey, McGraw, and Callahan met the King of England as all in the business of the day, and they found him a good fellow. They were entertained by the best-known people in each country. In Ceylon, so "Sam" Crawford, who was along, tells me, Sir Thomas Lipton showered hospitality on the travelers and made friends for life with every member of the party.

Several men who have been ball players have become wealthy through their connections with the game. Look at Charles Comiskey, who now owns the Chicago White Sox, one of the best money-making clubs in the country, because of the loyalty of Chicago fans to him. Governor Tener of Pennsylvania, and now also president of the National League, has acquired fame and position, and he started in life as a ball player. He has also made money, but not a fortune, of course. Then there is "Willie" Keeler, who saved his money and bought real estate in Brooklyn. He is comfortably off now and does not need to worry about the future. Fielder Jones, once the manager of the White Sox, retired from the game to go into business in the Northwest, he having developed this business in the winter months and with the money he got out of baseball. "Connie" Mack owns a large part of the Philadelphia American League Club, which stock furnishes him with a comfortable income besides the handsome salary he receives for managing the Athletics. "Ned" Hanlon is not broke, and John McGraw has considerable money, they tell me, although he can spend as fast as any man I ever saw work, and I have watched a lot of them. The money just seems to run through his fingers, and he is one of that isolated sort who does not care to let anyone else in his party spend anything at all.

Here is a strange thing. It may sound like a paradox, but the better salaries paid to ball players nowadays make them more thrifty. In the old days, when the salaries were poor, baseball was counted more as a frolic than a business, and most of the participants spent the money as fast as they could get it, so that by the time winter rolled around they were broke. Then they had to keep touching the club treasurer in the off season for advance money, so that they had eaten into their next season's salary before the first game had been played. They lived from hand to mouth, and the salaries were not large enough to make saving worth while. A ball player could work at saving for a long time and not show any very good results. Then the men in the game were less stable.

The pay of to-day is extremely good, and a player has a chance to live well and yet save and invest against the future. The Federal League has improved salaries, as a war always does, but I don't believe baseball is going to hold the present salary pace, although, of course, I hope it does, because the players benefit. I was signed up right after the world's series of 1913, before the Federal League broke out all over baseball like the prickly heat, and I am taking down very fair money even without using any outlaw offers as a wedge.

With the aid of the Federal League the salaries are jumping too fast, I believe, and the expenses increasing to a mark that is beyond what the game should stand. The magnates are not going to keep fighting one another very long when they are losing money, and I think that, if the Federals live, some sort of a consolidation will be made which will keep the salaries from jumping so fast.

There are certain natural qualifications required of a man before he can make good in the Big league. A boy cannot start out and say he is going to be a star ball player or even a Big Leaguer as he can make up his mind to become a doctor or a lawyer. A man with any sort of a physique can be a physician or lawyer, but the ball player must have a good physique. Most men enter the profession through an accident or rather luck. They play ball with amateurs and are picked up by a minor league team. Then some scout gets his eyes on the prospect, and he is taken South for a trial. That is the turning-point in the lives of all prospective Big Leaguers, because then they either must show or go back. Most of them turn back.

A doctor or a lawyer is usually in debt when he first starts out in his chosen profession, because, after years of preparation, the business of building up a practice and inspiring confidence is slow. A ball player gets good money from the jump and is not in debt, as a rule. Baseball is a healthy business, and there are the best conditioned men in the game, if you take the average, that there are in any business in the world, or sport either, for that matter. It is much better for a man physically than prizefighting, because it is not so strenuous and does not require such vigorous training. It is played outdoors and fighters, as a rule, work inside. Baseball does not strain a man as fighting or rowing or running does. When a man has good health, he is generally pretty happy even if he has not formed a trust and cornered some necessity of life, and even if he is not doling this necessity out at so much per dole.

Many men come into the major leagues without having had the opportunity to collect much education. I never went to college myself, although I expect to send my son when he reaches the proper age. Many of the ambitious ones go to college in the winter and use the money they have earned in the summer to get something which they could not afford when younger. Neither John McGraw nor Hugh Jennings had much education when they started playing baseball. Both went to St. Bonaventure College while they were with the Baltimore club, and the faculty in that institution is responsible for the statement that there never were two harder students than McGraw and Jennings, and that it wishes it could get a couple of Big Leaguers to attend each winter, since the other students admired the famous players and tried to imitate them, as is natural. The result was that the student average was much higher at St. Bonaventure while Jennings and McGraw attended.

Jennings went to the Cornell law school later and was admitted to the bar in Pennsylvania, where he practices some in the winter even yet. He also dived into the swimming tank at Cornell one day when there was no water in it and cracked his head on the tile bottom. The tank was so full of steam that Hugh did not know the water had been drained. For a time it looked as though Detroit was going to be forced to dig up a new manager, but Jennings finally came around.

"That's no way to kill me," said Jennings afterwards. "You've got to do something else besides try to break my neck, and I've got some ball players who would have broken the tile bottom if they had landed on their heads."

"Charley" Herzog, now the manager of Cincinnati and formerly the Giants' third baseman, has told me that he expects to go to Cornell some winter soon to take the agricultural course at that institution so that he will be better prepared to farm his Maryland preserve scientifically when he gets through with baseball. However, they say he is fairly scientific at farming now and makes a very handsome annual profit out of his efforts on the Maryland soil. He is another ball player who won't be forced to look for a job as a bartender or at some of those occupations which used to be so popular with the Big Leaguers when they wore out. "Charlie," they say, has done well at saving and is comfortably fixed.

XI. Is Baseball a Good Profession?

Until this Federal League outbreak, the salaries paid in baseball were not as big as was generally supposed from the accounts in the newspapers. But I happen to know that twenty-two men on a world's series contender which was defeated divided the losers' end a few seasons back and the average per man, if the pay-roll and the world's series money had been split up into twenty-two equal parts, would have been $6,100. Of course, some of the twenty-two received less money than this, as certain men on the club were high salaried, but I don't believe any member of this team took away less than $5,000 for his season's work, which covered a period of six months. This is a very fair return when compared to other salaries in other businesses. As I have said, the salaries in baseball before the Federal League raid were not as big as supposed, and it would have been almost possible to count on the fingers of the two hands the players in the American League who received more than $5,000 a season without including the world's series rake-off if a man were on a pennant winner, two years ago. But it must be looked at from another angle. Many of these men would be working in coal mines or at some occupation which would bring in only very low wages if they were not in the Big League. Ball clubs travel as well as anyone can travel, and the players are given the best of food, but I will have more to say about this in my next article, which will be about a team off the field.

Besides the income from baseball, many players make money on the side from sources which are the direct result of their baseball connections. For instance, Matthewson, Collins, and I have written more or less for the newspapers, and so have other players. Many ball players go into vaudeville. Frequently, advertising companies will pay to have some article, such as a razor, which is being pushed, indorsed by a well-known ball player. The Big Leaguers have learned to demand and get money for the use of their names in this way. We know that we must get the money quick.

It is my opinion that baseball as a profession, taken by and large, is still puffing along on the up grade. I do not doubt that the day will come when every Big League club will have a plant in the South in charge of experts, where the prospective youngsters will be educated and trained before they join the club. Many of the teams are approaching this now; the Giants have practically permanent quarters at Marlin, the White Sox at Paso Robles, in California, etc. Big Leaguers are becoming more and more a highly trained bunch of specialists.

Still, I would not advise a boy to make up his mind that he is going to be a Big League ball player. The chances are too strong against him making good. Managers receive hundreds of letters each season from prospects that are never answered. The managers have not the time to look up the authors. I believe there are many boys who would be stars if they had an opportunity that don't get jobs. Practically the only sure way for a youngster to attract the attention of a Big League manager is to get next to some friend of the manager to advance your name. Show some minor league manager what you can do, and, if he is convinced, his recommendation may carry you to the top.

In writing this article on baseball as a profession I have tried to be fair and keep my balance. If you make good, it is a fine profession. That is, it is good after you get in. And all this discussion applies to the Big Leagues. Playing ball in the minors is no business. My theory is that it never pays to be a "busher" in anything you do.

CHAPTER XII

Off the Field with the Big League Players

How the men in baseball spend their time when they are not "in the spangles." The peculiarities of various stars with which many of the fans are not acquainted. Some like moving picture shows and others the theaters. Still others prefer cards. What the big stars eat and how they live. This is a very interesting story because of the light it throws on the private lives of well-known Big Leaguers.

Most fans seem to believe that a ball player has nothing to spend except time. It is very generally figured that a Big Leaguer's period of labor covers about two hours every day, with no work on rainy days and a layoff on about half of the Sundays.

"I wish I had hours like yours," says the outsider. "It's an easy life, to take a little exercise in the afternoon and have the rest of the time to yourself."

To correct this impression I am going to show how ball players spend their time off the field and thereby try to convince those followers of the game who believe that the life of a Big Leaguer is practically the same as loafing that the playing of baseball entails some work besides that done on the diamond, and that style of careful living which does not fit in well with just plain loafing.

Arthur Shafer, third baseman of the Giants, gave out an interview recently in which he said he thought he would quit baseball because he had aged ten years since he had joined a Big League club, although his period of service has not extended over nearly as much time. As I recall it, Shafer joined the Giants in 1909. Shafer added, as another reason for retiring, that his hair had begun to turn gray, a fact that was doubtless discovered for him by his wife after he married, an event which took place in 1913. I believe that what the young third baseman of the Giants has said about aging and the gray hair coming in the Big League is true, but if he sticks to his announced determination to retire, I don't see how he is going to get along without the diet of excitement to which a few years of service in the Big League accustoms a man. I don't believe I could, but I am going to give it a try some day. That is the reason so few Big Leaguers ever stay retired, although many of them try it before they finally have the "spangles" cut off them.

If a fan thinks that a ball player is through with his day's work as soon as he takes off his uniform after a game, he should travel with a club for a time that is up in the battling for the pennant. The players never forget the game when the fight gets close, and many of a nervous temperament are unable to sleep.

Off the field, Jennings, our manager, does not keep a very close watch on the Detroit players to see that they confine their habits of life to the straight and narrow path. He believes that this should be left to the ball player himself, and that a man should have enough natural common sense to behave if he intends to make baseball his business, since this is the only way in which he can derive any profit from his enterprise. It is not until Jennings discovers a man misbehaving that he puts on the clamps and then look out for him. He knows how to treat a "bad actor" as well as anyone when he encounters one, since he played on the old Baltimore club, where the irresponsible players were plentiful.

There was an outfielder on the Detroit team a few seasons ago who had the habits of an owl, or at least he thought he had. Now there is a sort of unwritten law on all ball clubs that the players must be in bed by midnight when the team is on the road, and also when it is at home, too, for that matter, and Jennings does not like to have his men sleep after ten o'clock in the morning. "You'll get all the habits of an actor when you sleep until noon, and you are not wide awake by the time you should play ball," Jennings once told a player who liked to remain in the feathers up to the point where he just had time to get something to eat and then hustle for the ball park.

This outfielder I have in mind always used to say that he was afraid of a fire in a hotel, since he had been caught in one once while he was still in the bush league, and it was only his agility in escaping that had kept the Big League from losing a coming star. In fact, he was much prouder of his own stellar qualities than the rest of us. Because of this fear of fire, he would never go higher than the second floor of a hotel if he could help it. This made it easy for him to walk down or to take the fire escape route if he so desired. But the fear of fire was not his real reason for this attitude, as later developed.

Jennings found his man looking heavy eyed and falling off in his batting one season, and began to suspect that he was not taking the best of care of himself. Therefore, he set a watch on him to see that he went to bed in good time. When Jennings kicked to him about his sluggishness, he complained that he was ill.

"I believe," he said, "that I must have a touch of malaria, and it has taken all the 'pep' out of me."

One night this particular player, who had been loafing around the lobby of a hotel talking to Jennings, finally rose, stretched, yawned, and said:

"Well, me for the hay to see if I can't get back some of this old 'pep.'"

"That's the stuff," answered "Hughie," heartily.

The player walked to the elevator in full view of the manager and climbed aboard. After watching the elevator for a while, Jennings met some friends and went off to a quiet place where they fell to discussing baseball so vigorously that the meeting was not terminated until about four o'clock in the morning. While Jennings was waiting to ascend in the elevator in which the boy was sleeping while it was stopped at some upper story, he saw a familiar figure roll into the lobby. Jennings ducked behind one of those property palms that you find in every hotel lobby where the player could not see him. Then he waited until the wanderer had pushed the elevator button three or four times. At last, the boy was awakened, and the car appeared. Jennings slipped out from behind the palm and climbed into the elevator.

"Do you walk in your sleep?" inquired "Hughie," sardonically. "I thought you were going to the feathers about half-past ten."

"A friend of mine was sick and sent for me," answered the player.

"And you took the medicine along with him, judging by the few whiffs of your breath that I have caught," said Jennings. "Your little expedition is going to cost you a large fine and suspension."

It was not long afterwards that Jennings traded this man, but the story of his misbehavior never got into the newspapers, because Hugh is far too shrewd to spoil a deal by letting it become known that the material he expects to employ in the swapping is hard to handle. He was anxious as to how the player had made his exits, since the manager had watched the elevators carefully to see that the man did not come downstairs for an hour or two after he retired each night. It seems that he took to the freight elevator on some occasions, while he came down the stairs at other times. Hence his desire for a room on the second or third story, since this did not mean so many stairs to descend. Also, he was familiar with the availability of the fire escapes for his purposes. It seems that these afforded a fine and safe sort of exit, as he could come within a few feet of the ground on the ladders and then drop the rest of the way. He figured it dangerous to come down more than a story or two for fear that the occupants of the rooms whose windows he would pass in his journey would either mistake him for a burglar and shoot him or think that the hotel was on fire and give the alarm.

The Big Leaguer spends much of his time on the trains, and though ball clubs travel in great luxury, this constant traveling, nevertheless, is work. There are many methods of killing the time spent in travel in which is not included the observation of the passing scenery. Few of the men, after they have made one swing around the circuit, pay any attention to the scenery—that is, the scenery of nature.

On every ball team I ever saw, there is always a man who is either a comedian, or thinks he is. We had with the Detroit club for several years "Germany" Schaefer, one of the funniest men ever to enter the Big League, I believe. We missed him when he went to Washington, for "Dutch" passed many weary hours for us on the trains with his laugh producers. Rossman, the big Detroit first baseman, used to be another funny fellow.

I recall an incident which occurred in a game against the Athletics some years ago when both Rossman and Schaefer were on the Detroit club, and which has nothing to do with the habits of a ball club off the field, but which is a sample of the Schaefer brand of comedy. Big Rossman, who had a terrible wallop with the bat, won a game for us in the ninth inning with a blow over the fence. As soon as the ball was hit, and "Germany" got a glance at its general direction and carrying possibilities, he seized a towel out of the hand of the club trainer, ran from where he was on the bench, and followed the big first baseman from the time he turned the first bag around to the home plate, fanning him with the towel as they progressed. It was only necessary for the pair to jog to reach home in safety.

"Well, we made it," puffed Schaefer when they arrived. Then he put up his hand to the umpire for silence. "My run don't count," he announced to the press stand, "but we don't need it."

Many ball players indulge in cards, and the newspaper correspondents who travel with the club join in these games. They are for small stakes, as a rule, and poker is the favorite medium for the exchange of money, although there are usually four or five bridge players on every team who sit silently fingering their cards. Jennings has no objection to the men on his team playing poker if they do not start a game late at night and sit up past the bed hour in order to "go just one more round." The only manager I ever heard of barring poker entirely was McGraw when his team won the championship of the National League in a whirlwind finish on its final tour through the West in 1911. As I hear the story, the members of the Giants had been playing a pretty stiff game that summer and some of the boys were inclined to brood over their losses when they were hit especially hard. This served to take their minds off baseball, and so McGraw stopped the cards for the final trip. Cards were tabooed only on that important trip.

However, the Giants' manager, along with all the other leaders, objects to poker games that result in the players sitting up far into the night. A season or two ago, McGraw, who has easy notions similar to those of Jennings in his supervision over the players on points of training, found several of his men, including two or three of the wise old veterans on the club, playing poker at two o'clock in the morning. One of the men in the game was a youngster who was serving his first year with a Big League club. When McGraw entered the room, which had been assigned to two of the veterans, this busher hastily poured his chips into his pocket and denied he had taken part as McGraw began to plaster on the fines. He declared he had been only looking on.

"You'll get just twice as big a plaster as the others," announced "Mack," as he stepped up to the man and hit him on the pocket, out of which the chips were bulging. "If you had not lied to me, there would not have been any fine at all for you, because I would have believed the older men were responsible for your presence."

McGraw was as good as his word and let the other recruit who was in the party off with a reprimand but no fine. The veterans had to stand a nick in the bank roll, however, and so did the youngster who had lied.

But you take baseball as a whole now, and you'll find practically no "bad actors" in it as the term was formerly applied. Managers do not have to keep as close watch on their players as they did once, because the men themselves are smart enough to appreciate the fact that they cannot keep up with the speed of the Big League, and bat around all night. There is only one recent rumor of lack of training which has hurt a team very extensively, and I am not sure that this is true. My information comes from the American Leaguers in the same city where this National League club is located, and they have told me that the loose habits of some of the men on the club in the rival league were largely responsible for the team dropping back after it looked as if it had a good chance to win the pennant.

There was some talk that one or two of "Connie" Mack's players did not stick close to the training rules in 1912, and that this lack of condition on the part of some of the tars had cost the club the league championship. You will find it is true that any time a man with a reputation falls down during a season, the report will spread rapidly that he is not observing the rules of training. As a matter of fact, I do not believe that any of the men on the Athletics who were supposed to have been careless about their condition broke the training rules to any extent. It was just an off season for the team as a whole and some of the stars in particular. One man who was charged with training irregularities had just purchased his first automobile after being a member of the winning team in the world's series the previous fall, and I have been told that he was inclined to stay out rather late in this at times. But do not believe all you hear about a player running wild when he has a bad season. This is always the charge, and we must all have our off years.

Most managers do not forbid players to smoke cigarettes unless some of the men are overdoing it. Both the Giants and Athletics smoke cigarettes if they want to, but Fred Clarke, of the Pirates, stopped his players from doing this last season on the theory that cigarettes were bad for the wind. The elimination of them did not seem to speed the club up any, for it is the gossip of the game that the slowness of the Pirates is their big weakness. Branch Rickey, the new manager of the St. Louis Browns, has introduced a novel system to induce his players to lay off cigarettes. He has arranged for the club to supply the players with cigars. Any time one of the men desires to smoke, he goes to Rickey and asks him for a cigar. Perhaps this feature has been added with the idea that more men will be inclined to go to that club willingly. It might be considered as almost a bribe. Also, I'll bet the friends of the players are well supplied.

Personally, I don't smoke cigarettes, but I usually smoke about three cigars a day in season and out, and they do not seem to hurt me at all. Mathewson has told me that he generally cuts out tobacco from the time he goes South for spring training until the season opens. This is just with the idea of giving himself a rest from it once a year. He smokes pretty frequently during the baseball season, but mostly cigars.

My habits during the season are fairly regular. My rising hour is about half past nine or ten, so that I am through my breakfast by half past ten or eleven. Then I generally loaf around the hotel and read the newspapers for an hour or so, unless I have some business to attend to in the city where we happen to be playing. For a time, I used to rise a little earlier and play a round of golf, but I discovered that the Scotch game was hurting my batting, and I refuse to toy with anything that affects the old hitting, because that is my stock-in-trade. By half past two each afternoon, I am out at the ball park and in uniform and on the field by three where the team indulges in practice.

I never eat any lunch, as I feel that it makes me loggy for the game, and it is important that I be in shape. That is my business— being in shape. A few of the players take some light lunch, such as broth or milk and crackers, but they are the ones whose habit it is to rise earlier than I do, and they feel that they need the nourishment for strength. None of the regulars eats heavily at noon. Sometimes we will get a busher who runs his eye over the menu and thinks he sees great opportunities. He goes after the food and generally makes a bad impression at the ball park if he gets a chance to show. As I have said before, many a youngster has eaten himself right out of the Big League.

As a matter of fact, I never eat any lunch even in the winter when I am at my home in Augusta, where I retire and rise early. On my hunting expeditions, I pass up lunch except perhaps for a sandwich, and I believe that the ordinary man would find himself in better physical shape if he would try the two-meal-a-day diet. It is an easy one to get accustomed to, and it certainly makes a man enjoy his dinner.

A newspaper friend of mine came to Augusta last fall to pay me a visit and to do a little hunting with me. He had been accustomed to the Big Town and was used to having lunch. The first day that I told him I hoped he did not count on lunch, because none was served in my house, he looked kind of downcast, and I took him downtown to a restaurant, where he tackled enough food to do me for a dinner. It was not three or four days, though, before he had become used to only two meals, and he developed twice as much pepper on the diet as he had displayed when he first arrived. He has written me frequently since his visit, and he informs me that he lives right along on two meals a day now, and has not been threatened with starving to death so far. He adds that he never felt better in his life and that he has been in perfect health all winter. He has also converted some of his friends, and his instituted quite a movement for two meals a day which has caught on and spread. As a matter of fact, I don't see how any man, who is confined to an office for eight or nine hours each day, and who gets very little exercise, can expect to eat three meals and show any pepper. It just clogs the system all up with too much fuel and reduces the efficiency. In automobile parlance, it gives too rich a mixture.

After each game, the fan sees the last of the players rushing for the clubhouse no matter how tired they all may be. That is the habit of a Big Leaguer. But the dash does not stop when the threshold of the clubhouse is crossed. Not on your life. It is born into every Big Leaguer, after he has been in the fast society for a time, to rush at everything he does. Therefore, all the boys dress as rapidly as they can and dig for the hotel, when on the road, where they hurtle themselves into the dining room and abuse the waiter if he does not rush on the food with the speed of a sprinter. It is the nervous energy wearing off. All through a game, a player is keyed up to concert pitch, and this strain breaks after the battle.

The first relaxation comes after dinner, when you will generally find the man who was hastening most to grab his meal loafing around the lobby doing nothing. But when a ball player has something on his mind to be done, he always wants to accomplish it with a rush. It is the same with boarding a train. They all dash into the coaches and rush for their berths as if the berths were going to move away if they did not flop into them quick. They get sore if there is some hitch in the arrival of their baggage, but train wrecks do not feaze [sic] veterans to any great extent.

After dinner, many of the players go to the theaters, while some go to moving picture shows. We are usually invited to different shows when we go to play a town, which reduces the cost of living. After the theater, it is home and bed. It is evident from this outline of the habits of a Big Leaguer that he has not much idle time on his hands. This does not take into consideration the hard jumps, when a club will travel for a day and two nights on a sleeper and then get out to play one game or perhaps a double header. Toward the end of the season, when there are frequently odd contests to be played off, a team may be forced to spend several nights in succession in a sleeper and play ball every day besides. I don't care what anybody may say, I know that a man cannot get the rest in a Pullman that he acquires in a stationary bed.

I said that I do not eat any lunch. Perhaps it would interest the reader to know in detail what some of the stars in our league do about lunch, so I will dwell on the habits of a few of those whom I know. Walter Johnson is a great boy to eat ice cream, and you will find him consuming a big plate of it most every day about noon time. Baker is the one exception to the lunch rule. He has always lived on a farm and is accustomed to the early to bed and early to rise theory, so he gets up bright and smart even in the season when the club is on the road. Members of the Athletics say that "Bake" hates the road anyway. He will sit down and eat a heavy lunch and go out and play baseball in the afternoon, and a whole lot of it. "Eddie" Collins is a great consumer of chocolate ice cream, and he also likes broth. "Eddie" Plank will eat a little soup when he expects to work in the afternoon. I ate lunch with Christy Mathewson one day last fall during the world's series, and he confined himself to a plate of soup and a chocolate éclair.

I have heard a funny story about "Eddie" Collins. He was in New York toward the end of the season last year when the Athletics had cinched the pennant, and he went out to lunch with some friends of his, and they insisted that he eat heartily. He partook of some soup, a nice large slice of roast beef, a few potatoes, and some chocolate ice cream.

"You'll never be able to play ball after that amount of food," proclaimed his host.

"Don't you think so?" laughed the somewhat bashful and extremely modest Collins.

"I'll tell you what I'll do," challenged the host. "I'll bet anyone present that he doesn't get a hit and that he makes an error after that big lunch."

"I'll take you," said two other members of the party.

"Eddie" got something like seven chances that afternoon, one a very difficult one, and he never made a misplay. He also collected three hits. Still, this anecdote is no boost for a heavy meal in the middle of the day, but it is rather the old exception which proves the rule.

Ball players who are not fortunate enough to belong to one of the teams taking part in the world's series have the most fun at that time of the season, because they have not the nervous strain of the games on their minds constantly. However, if you ask me for my opinion, I prefer to carry the nervous strain. During the rainy spell which interrupted the world's series between the Giants and the Athletics for several days in 1911, a party of us, including several newspaper men, Sherwood Magee, and "Germany" Schaefer, went to a place in Philadelphia which has since closed its door. However, it was then one of those society centers where the table tops are covered with oil-cloth and all the talent is supplied by the patrons. Never a night passed there that some member of a party did not arise and recite "The Face on the Barroom Floor," which is a general signal for pulling down the shutters.

Schaefer was requested to sing that night, and "Germany" has a voice which cannot be distinguished from the general tone and hoarseness of a tugboat's whistle. However, "Shaef" accepted the challenge and uncorked the "Wearing of the Green." It was possible to recognize it only by listening to the words, and if this is libel, let Schaefer make the most of it. After Schaefer had rendered the song, of course, there was a burst of applause, and he threatened to be a "riot," as the vaudeville performers say, an expression which I learned from my brief experience on the stage. "Germany" extended his hands to indicate that he demanded silence. When finally the applause had subsided, he said:

"Gentlemen and Ladies. Would you believe that two years ago I could not sing a note? Now experts tell me that 'Sammy' Strang has nothing on me."

"Sammy" Strang, for the benefit of those who don't know, was a Big League ball player, but he quit the game some time ago to study abroad for grand opera. This is a sample of the spontaneity of the Schaefer wit.

Let me emphasize one point I brought up earlier in the story. When you hear that a player is cutting loose in his living don't believe it. This story was once circulated about a whole team after it had lost a world's series when it went into the first game a ruling favorite. The report was that the players were so sure of a victory that they had been up all the night before the first game playing cards and drinking beer by way of a premature celebration. I happen to know that there was absolutely no foundation for such a yarn. Baseball is the most gossipy game in the world.

McGraw has a good system to insure the early retiring of his players when the team is at home, a problem that has baffled many managers because the players are scattered. He insists that every man report in the clubhouse at the Polo Grounds by ten o'clock in the morning. Nobody can show up at that hour bright eyed if he has been misbehaving the night before. A big fine awaits the absentee the first time, a bigger one the second, and McGraw does not care where a fine drops. After the team is well started on its season, he does not even make the regulars put on their uniforms, but they must be on hand for the morning roll call.

Index

Index

Index